THE CONSISTENT TRADER

How to Build a Winning Trading System, Master Your Psychology, and Earn Consistent Profits in the Forex Market

SAM EDER

ISBN: 978-1-63161-025-7

Published by TCK Publishing

www.TCKPublishing.com

Get discounts and special deals on our best selling books at

www.TCKPublishing.com/bookdeals

TABLE OF CONTENTS

FREE ONLINE COURSE AND INTERACTIVE WORKSHEETS

This book is accompanied by an online course with videos, interactive worksheets and additional resources to help you develop your trading skills.

If you watch the videos and do the worksheets as you go through the book your learning experience will be that much greater.

All the material is free, so go ahead and sign-up for access.

www.fxrenew.com/forex-course

Disclaimer

The following is meant for informational purposes only. Please consult your investment advisor before trading Forex.

THE ROAD MAP TO THE CONSISTENT TRADER

"I believe anyone can do this job; I don't think you have to be born to do it."

~ Stuart Walton

Welcome to **The Consistent Trader**.

Why do I focus on consistency?

Firstly, if you can produce consistent profits, it can make a measurable difference in your life. A 20-30% return on your capital per year (2-3% a month) from active Forex trading significantly adds up over your lifetime. While larger returns are certainly possible—and you will learn more about how to achieve them in this book—consistent returns are highly desirable.

Secondly, consistent trading is *easier*. If you are consistently winning, it's easier to both build and operate your trading systems. You will trade in a more relaxed and happy manner and ultimately make fewer mistakes, which is highly desirable, because mistakes kill trading systems.

Thirdly, it's a "scientific process". If you include the elements of **The Consistent Trader** in your trading plan, you will go from trading failure to success in a step-by-step manner. There is no guesswork here. All you must do is follow a disciplined process that will take your trading to a point where you are achieving your financial goals each and every year.

In this book, we go through several lessons on how to be a consistent trader. These include:

- How to identify the market type so you can trade the correct strategy for the current conditions

- How to find damn-good set-ups to increase your winning probability

- How to stalk a low-risk/high-reward entry point

- How to set proper objectives

- How to build a position-sizing model to achieve your objectives

- How to protect yourself from losses with a hard-to-hit stop-loss

- How to trade the market that is in front of you with a complex exit strategy

- How to stay calm and be mistake free for perfect order execution

THE MARKET WIZARDS

In 1989, Jack Schwager released his first book in a series of four containing interviews with some of the best traders and investors of the time. It was *titled Market Wizards: Interviews with Top Traders.* Since then, traders and investors who have been interviewed in Schwager's books have been given the title "Market Wizard."

Throughout this book, you will find quotes from these Market Wizards, as well as guidance on how to apply their best practices and principles to Forex Trading. I credit one of these "Wizards"—Dr. Van K. Tharp—in particular, and both he and the other Market Wizards have had a huge influence on my development as a trader. I owe them a debt of gratitude for sharing their thoughts and insights.

DOWNLOAD THE INTERACTIVE FOREX TRADING SYSTEM TEMPLATE

Throughout the book, you will be working on your trading plan.

To help you do this, we provide you with an interactive trading plan template called "My Trading System", which will ultimately tell you:

- What to trade
- How much to trade
- When to trade
- When to exit the trade

You can download and print the Forex Trading System template for free when you subscribe to my free course:

www.fxrenew.com/forex-course

This book is made up of just over twenty chapters and broken into roughly three sections, which are as follows:

FOUNDATIONS OF STRENGTH

"The realization that you are responsible for your results is the key to successful investing. Winners know they are responsible for their results; losers think they are not."

~ Van Tharp

In the first section of this book, you will begin your transformation into an accomplished Forex Trader. You will learn how your beliefs shape your trading and how to change your beliefs into those of a top trader. You will develop a model of the market that guides decision-making, and you will develop extreme clarity in your Forex trading goals and objectives.

The importance of foundations cannot be overstated. It is possible to jump straight into building a winning Forex trading system without them, but most people who do this eventually make mistakes that cost them all their profits and then some. Importantly, people who trade without building a good foundation tend to *ask the wrong questions*. They don't think like top traders, setting themselves up for failure and not success.

By developing the foundational skills of objective setting and risk management, by cultivating a knowledge of risk/reward, statistics, and probabilities, and by understanding what works and what doesn't, you automatically put yourself in the top percentage of market participants. This makes building and maintaining a profitable Forex trading system much easier over the long-term. Anyone can get lucky in Forex and make one or two good trades, but you want to have a winning system that works year after year after year.

BUILDING A WINNING FOREX TRADING SYSTEM

"Frankly, I don't see markets; I see risks, rewards, and money."

~ Larry Hite

In this section, we take a step-by-step approach to building a winning Forex trading system. This starts with defining market types. Expecting the same trading system to work in all types of markets is a fool's hope and a common trading mistake. You will learn how to get an edge over the market through different set-ups and how to implement trades and time your entries and exits for maximum gain.

Finally, you will learn how to use position sizing to achieve your objectives, along with advanced trade-management techniques that greatly improve your consistency as a trader.

Developing the Master Trader Mindset

"Pride is a great banana peel—as are hope, fear, and greed. My biggest slip-ups occurred shortly after I got emotionally involved with positions."

~ Ed Seykota

In the final part of the book, we focus on your trading psychology. This is to prepare you to execute your systems mistake-free, even when you have large amounts of money on the line.

Mistakes kill trading systems, and the more money on the line, the greater the impact that mistake will have on your financial future. Your job as a trader, once you have built your winning trading system, is to execute it flawlessly.

The Master Trader Mindset encompasses the tasks needed for perfect execution of your trading plan, how to run your trading business professionally, and how to get into the trading "zone". Trading successes is about your psychology as a trader, and this section of the book will equip you with the tools you need to succeed throughout your trading career.

This Is a Book You Can Read More Than Once

To make the most of this book, you will find it helpful to read it several times.

As you become more experienced, you will find that what you read will have a different meaning. Don't be shy to re-read or refer to sections of this book again and again.

Additionally, if you are having trouble grasping a concept the first time around, don't stress. Note it down, and come back to it again later. Trading is an in-depth and oftentimes quite subtle topic, so don't pressure yourself into learning everything all in one go. Relax!

PERSISTENCE IS A KEY TRAIT OF A WINNING TRADER

When you begin reading a book, you are typically full of enthusiasm, but as life takes a hold again it can be challenging to maintain that momentum.

Exercises don't get done, or they get skipped. You skim read, instead of taking the time to do things properly, or you move on to the next shiny thing, and the book gets left to gather dust on the shelf.

In any case, the wisdom you could have gleaned is lost, and the transformation you could have achieved simply never happens.

DON'T MAKE THAT MISTAKE WITH THIS BOOK

This book will have an incredible impact on your financial future. I could show you fancy charts and projections in an Excel spreadsheet, but to suggest that following the steps in this book could be worth hundreds of thousands of dollars over your trading lifetime is not an understatement.

Say each chapter takes a minimum of 2 hours to read and add into your trading plan. Then suppose that over a lifetime of trading—which could last for fifty years or more!—you make $100,000 more by reading this book than you would make if you didn't. That makes each hour you spend on this book worth $2500! For some people, this is going to be significantly more, depending on their trading stake. When you're feeling discouraged, distracted, or overwhelmed, keep this motivation in mind.

Finally, don't forget to get your interactive trading system template when you subscribe to my free course here:

www.fxrenew.com/forex-course

HOW BELIEFS SHAPE YOUR TRADING

"You don't trade the markets – you trade your beliefs about the markets."

~ Van Tharp

As a Forex trader, you have the freedom to make your own decisions. You are not constrained by schoolteachers, bosses, or parents. You operate in what is essentially an "unlimited environment". No one is forcing you to trade like a parent forces you to go to bed or your manger forces you be at work at a certain time!

This lack of restriction can be a double-edged sword. While you have the freedom to do as you please, this lack of structure can cause you to make mistakes. Therefore, you need to build a set of rules that guide your behavior in the markets.

The creation of these rules starts with your beliefs. In the markets, beliefs act as filters for your actions. When you add a rule to your trading plan, it is because you believe that rule will help provide you with a trading edge.

Your beliefs greatly impact your Forex trading. For example:

- If you believe Forex Trading is risky, you may not place trades when you should
- If you believe in a chart pattern, you might place a trade
- If you believe in not taking losses, you might not use a stop-loss
- If you believe in a fundamental story, you might place a trade
- If you believe Forex trading is difficult, you might find it difficult
- If you believe Forex trading is easy, you might not take it seriously

These belief statements are not judgments. They are simply the way you operate, rightly or wrongly.

YOUR BELIEFS GUIDE YOU ALONG THE ROCKY PATHS

"Many people actually want to lose on a subconscious level."

~ Van Tharp

Your beliefs guide you on the decisions you make with your money. But chances are, your beliefs have never been optimized for trading, and many of them may be counterproductive. For example, they may:

- Cause you to hold on to a losing position to avoid taking a "loss"

- Overtrade on your account and pay away your profits to your broker

- Close winning positions too quickly, instead of holding on for the big wins

Some beliefs are difficult to let go of. These beliefs may have developed out of a painful or formative experience or are perhaps ingrained in your culture as accepted wisdom. But the wonderful thing about being human is that ultimately, you can make a conscious choice to change. Once you recognize you have a belief, you can change it. You can upgrade. And if you choose to renew your beliefs, why not choose the very best ones for trading success?

To find the very best trading beliefs, you can look to the master traders who have come before you. Unlike throughout most of history, we now have the luxury to look at the very best in our chosen field and model what they do.

YOU CAN WEAR BELIEFS LIKE YOU WEAR A HAT

"Truth – more precisely, an accurate understanding of reality – is the essential foundation for producing good outcomes."

~ Ray Dalio

Perhaps the most important point in this chapter is that not only can you choose your beliefs, you can also choose them purely because they are the most useful beliefs to hold at the time. For example, if you are skeptical about this concept and the impact beliefs have on your Forex trading, then perhaps try on this belief for size: *By having the beliefs of successful traders, I will be safer and smarter with my trading decisions.*

Be prepared to try on beliefs the same way you might try on hats. Keep the ones that fit and that provide a benefit to your Forex trading, and discard the others. You can even put a belief "aside" for a while, say a week, and then bring it back again. Keep testing and trying on new beliefs until you find the ones that work for you and help you to achieve your goals.

How to Change Your Beliefs

Changing your beliefs can be easy or it can be difficult. First, you The path become aware of your existing beliefs, and then you learn new beliefs that may be more useful for you. You can change some beliefs simply by learning a new and better belief. If you learn about a new belief in this book and decide to adopt it, then it becomes part of you.

Occasionally, there are beliefs that are difficult to change. These are often emotionally charged—or stuck—beliefs. You can tell this by the level of resistance you have to changing the belief. If you notice you feel as if you don't want to change a particular belief because the thought of changing it makes you angry, or the belief causes you losses in the market, then perhaps it is a stuck belief. These beliefs may require more work, and I suggest you read Van K. Tharp's *Trading Beyond the Matrix* to learn more in-depth techniques for dealing with these tricky beliefs. Remember, resistance to changing beliefs could be a sign you have a belief that needs changing. Be very self-aware anytime you have resistance.

WHAT ARE YOUR BELIEFS ABOUT THE MARKET?

"I think investment psychology is by far the more important element."

~ Tom Basso

In the next chapter, we will list the beliefs of top traders, but first, you need to gain awareness of your beliefs. The first step is to list your beliefs about the market. Don't think too much about what to write or not to write. Simply write down every belief or thought that comes into your mind when you think about Forex trading.

Here is a list of common beliefs from some of my students to help get you started:

You can download *a worksheet here* to help you with this exercise.

- If I hold my Forex trades for the long term, I will make money.

- Losses are bad

- Losses are good

- I need at least a risk/reward of 3:1 on each trade

- I don't know how to trade Forex

- If I learn technical analysis, I will be able to make money from Forex trading

- The markets are impossible to predict over the long term

- The markets are impossible to predict over the short term

- I don't trust my broker

- I should have 10% of my portfolio in Forex trading

- I have plenty of time until retirement

- I am financially free

- Chart indicators work in some situations but not in others

- I should buy the AUD

- Risk management is important

Once you have written down your beliefs, you must ask the following question of each statement:

"How do I benefit from having this belief?"

For example, I might analyze the belief, "I only need to know technical analysis to trade Forex because the fundamentals are too hard to predict." When I ask, "What do I get from this belief?" I came up with:

- I can avoid following the news

- I can keep my trading simple

- I need to learn more about technical analysis

- I can follow what my favorite "guru" says about Forex trading, which also makes me feel comfortable

- I can be very precise and disciplined in my Forex Trading

- I can back-test my charts easily

By listing your beliefs and asking this question, you start to become self-aware, an essential characteristic of the winning trader. You begin to see how the beliefs you have run your life and your Forex trading. You can also decide if a belief is useful to you or not.

Once you have awareness of your current beliefs, the next step is to gain knowledge of a new set of beliefs: the beliefs of top traders. With this knowledge you can then pick and choose what beliefs you wish to keep, and decide which new beliefs might serve you better.

If you have not done so already, use the *worksheet* to list as many beliefs as you can. Some people are able to do this exercise with ease, while others struggle to find beliefs to list. Either way, it is okay. Simply do your best, and realize that resistance and pain are signs you are growing.

HOW TO MODEL THE BELIEFS OF TOP TRADERS

"Understand that learning the market can take years. Immerse yourself in the world of trading and give up everything else. Get as close to other successful traders as you can. Consider working for one for free."

~ Linda Raschke

Within each of us is a top trader waiting to be unleashed.

The challenges are that they are buried under a weight of beliefs that have built up over a lifetime. Moving beyond these beliefs two simple things:

- Awareness
- Knowledge

The first step toward awakening the trader within is to become aware. You need to recognize the beliefs you have, know they a product of your personal history, and realize that perhaps there are better beliefs more suited to successful Forex Trading that you can choose to have.

Like Neo in the 1999 sci-fi film *The Matrix*, everything changes once you realize that your beliefs are simply a construct, a prison within the mind. You can then rise above your beliefs, and make your own rules for the game.

"There is no spoon."

~ Boy to Neo

The second step in awakening the trader within requires gaining knowledge. In *The Matrix*, Neo had a guide, Morpheus, played by Lawrence Fishburne. Morpheus taught Neo a new set of beliefs that tore down his restraints. It took time for Neo to believe, but when he did, he became free of limitation and was able to defy the laws of the world that had previously held him captive.

Here, you are like Neo, the student. After reading chapter 1, you know your existing beliefs; you have awareness. In this chapter, you will learn the new rules of the game; you will gain knowledge.

It's time to take the red pill and, like Neo, journey down the rabbit hole, and see how far into Wonderland you are willing to go.

FINDINGS FROM A MASTER'S THESIS IN LEADERSHIP

In 2009, I completed a master's thesis in Leadership. Before we move into more specific beliefs, it will be instructive to explore two of the key findings from this study.

My thesis subject was:

TOP LEADERS AND TOP TRADERS: AN EXPLORATION INTO WHY THEY SUCCEED

The crux of this study was that:

"Top leaders and traders share some common traits. In particular, they have a high degree of emotional intelligence and are engaged in self-study. They are able to formulate a plan that is right for them or their organization and stick to it with rigid discipline and confidence. Furthermore, when facts change and the plan needs adjusting, they are able to recognize this and adapt."

EMOTIONAL INTELLIGENCE IS MORE IMPORTANT THAN RAW INTELLIGENCE

The perception can be that top traders are number wizzes. But that is far from the truth. While it is important to understand some basic probabilities—trading is ultimately a statistical game—the more important skill is emotional intelligence (EQ).

From the study:

"Emotional intelligence includes factors such as self-awareness, self-discipline, empathy, and individual differences in the processing and regulation of emotions."

Basically, the better you are at controlling your emotions in the market, the more successful you will be. If you are here for the thrill of it, then you are unlikely to remain consistent over the long-term.

CONFIDENCE BREEDS DISCIPLINE

A second finding from the study is that you need to learn to trust yourself. You need to be confident in your approach to the markets.

When you are confident and trust in your Forex trading system, then you won't have any trouble remaining disciplined in following your plan.

Here is what Marty Schwartz, Market Wizard and author of *Pitbull: Lessons from Wall Street's Champion Day Trader* has to say.

"CONFIDENCE IS ESSENTIAL TO A SUCCESSFUL TRADER."

When dealing with a losing streak, Schwartz would trade a smaller size to make little profits:

"It's all psychological. I felt sick, and I wanted to make myself feel good again. I wanted to regain my confidence..."

During the losing streak, his fear of losing was slowing down his reaction time, making him take more risk.

"What happens is that as your fear of losing rises, your emotions start to short circuit your intellect, and you no longer have confidence in what you are doing."

Once he regained his confidence he was able to get the profits flowing again.

If you can regulate your emotions and remain confident while practicing the beliefs of top traders, you will be more than just a successful trader; you will have awakened the Forex trading giant within.

THE BELIEFS OF TOP TRADERS

"I knew I wanted it more than anybody else. There was no way I was not going to make it. I always had that competitive drive, whether it was getting into a top college, or competing in college sports."

~ *Jimmy Balodimas*

Listed below are the beliefs of top traders that we cover in this book. This is not meant to be a comprehensive list. Individual top traders will have plenty of beliefs that are not on this list. From my studies, I have noticed that several of these beliefs are common across many top traders, and some beliefs—like taking responsibility—are common to all top traders.

More importantly, if you model the majority of these beliefs, you will develop a powerful Forex trading belief structure that will last you a lifetime. You will become capable of enlightened decision-making when it comes to your Forex trading.

It's like riding a bike. Once you learn these skills, you won't lose them. You may fall off the bike every once in a while, but you will get right back on. You will be free from "conventional wisdom" forever. For some of you, the beliefs below might seem unclear at first. For some of you, they will be readily apparent. Either way, it is okay as you will learn them in detail in this book..

This is not an exhaustive list of beliefs. Rather, these are ones we cover in this book, and they form a good starting place for your development as a trader. Throughout the rest of this book, you will learn more about each belief and it's practical application in your Forex trading account.

TOP TRADERS BELIEVE THEY ARE RESPONSIBLE FOR THEIR OWN RESULTS

The cornerstone of an effective approach to trading is responsibility. By taking responsibility for your profits and losses, you gain control over your financial destiny.

It is easy to look for others to blame, be it your money manager, Forex broker, or even the market itself. By accepting that *you* are the ultimate determining factor in your success, you gain the ability to work on yourself and improve the way you trade.

TOP TRADERS BELIEVE IN HAVING IN-DEPTH OBJECTIVES

They have clearly defined goals.

You should know the reason you are trading. Perhaps you are looking for an early retirement on the beach (nice!) or would like to help a loved one live a better life (nicer!). These powerful motivations keep you from straying "off the beaten track" and help you trade with discipline.

Once you have uncovered your greater purpose, you can then define a goal (i.e., 10% a month and I don't want my account to be down more than 5%). Once you have these objectives, you can work out how much to trade in order to help you meet them. More on that later.

TOP TRADERS BELIEVE THAT TRADING IS A STATISTICAL GAME AND UNDERSTAND POSITIVE EXPECTANCY

Good traders know the outcome of any one trade is not 100% predictable. Rather, they seek to have a profit over a series of trades. Some trades are going to lose, and some will win. What matters is that, overall, the profit from the wining trades is greater than the losses from the losing trades.

TOP TRADERS BELIEVE IN APPROPRIATELY TAKING RISKS IN ORDER TO ACHIEVE THEIR GOALS

Acceptance of risk is a challenge for many traders. They would (of course!) prefer that they could make money without ever having to lose any. But losses are a fact of life in the markets. Accepting this fact is a positive thing. It frees you to create a trading plan that lets you move toward your goals.

To further illustrate this concept, trading psychologist and Market Wizard Van Tharp explained how changing his perception of risk tolerance was important in growing his company's retirement account.

Tharp shifted his tolerance for risk in his company retirement account. Previously, his goal had been to never have a losing year. He then established a new rule that allowed him to risk the chance of a 25% drawdown on the account, but only if the trading opportunity was A-grade.

By doing this, he was able to heavily purchase a silver stock that was trading for below the amount of cash it had in the bank, let alone the value of the silver it had in the ground. The stock quickly rose from $3 to $11 while he was invested, giving him the best year he had ever had.

If he had not accepted the risk of a 25% drawdown on his account, he would have never been able to capitalize on the opportunity as he did. (This is not an avocation to take such a big risk on a trade—it's the mind-set that matters).

TOP TRADERS BELIEVE THAT THEY SHOULD TRADE DIFFERENTLY IN DIFFERENT MARKET TYPES

Would you trade the same way in a bull market as you would in a bear market? Or the same way in a trending market as in a range-bound market?

Successful traders don't. One of their core habits is to identify the current market type first. Once they know what the current market type is, they adjust their strategy appropriately. Furthermore, they are aware that the market type could change at any time, and they are well prepared for the shift.

Top Traders Believe That They Achieve Their Goals through Position Sizing(Money Management), Not through Their Entries

Position sizing means knowing exactly how much you are risking on each trade, so you can achieve your objectives. It is based off the historical performance of your trading system for the current market type.

Successful traders know their goals and their expected performance and decide how much to trade based on this understanding.

Top Traders Believe They Have an Edge Over the Markets

An edge is an advantage that, over time, will provide you with healthy profits from the market. All successful traders have established an edge over the markets.

Examples of edges that successful traders have include:

- Technical analysis
- Fundamental analysis
- Getting trading advice from someone with an edge.

Top Traders Believe in Having a Simple Entry Strategy

Take a successful trader and an amateur trader. One is complex. The other is simple. But perhaps not in the way you might think.

The successful trader has a subtle, insightful, and in-depth trading plan, but he or she has rules for entering the market that allow him or her to act decisively when necessary.

An over-complicated set of entry criteria can confuse the trader just when they need to be decisive.

TOP TRADERS BELIEVE IN COMPLEX EXITS

While they value simplicity, successful traders will have many reasons to exit from a trade.

For example, they may have:

- An initial stop-loss
- A profit objective when they enter the trade
- A trailing stop to protect profits while in the trade
- A risk/reward stop to ensure the trade makes sense
- A different trailing stop that comes into play if the market type changes
- A time-stop if their idea is not working out

These exits all serve to maximize profits and minimize losses.

TOP TRADERS BELIEVE IN LETTING THEIR PROFITS RUN

An oldie but a goodie. One of the habits of successful traders is to let their profits run.

If you are in a good trade, don't be tempted to take your profit quickly. Use a method that protects your gains and at the same time allows you to capture big wins if the trade does go well for you.

Top Traders Believe in Cutting Losses Short

The flipside of letting your profits run is cutting short your losses.

Successful traders see losing trades as a "cost of doing business" and are quick to realize any losses.

Amateurs will do anything to avoid taking a loss, including holding on to a big losing position.

Top Traders Believe in Understanding the Risk/Reward Ratio Before They Enter Into a Trade

A cardinal habit of the successful trader is checking the risk/reward of a trade before entering into a position. If it is not favorable, then they won't place the trade.

For example, you may want to have a risk/reward of at least 1:2 on any individual trade, meaning your potential profit from the trade should be twice as big as your potential loss. This means that if you only get 50% of your trades correct, you would still have a winning Forex trading system. There are plenty of factors that go into selecting the correct risk/reward requirements from your strategy. We will cover these later in this book.

Top Traders Believe That It Is Okay to Lose More Often Than They Win, As Long As the Profits from the Wins Are Greater Than the Losses from the Losing Trades

It's not how often you lose that matters, it's how much you make when you win.

I'm going to leave this section to the esteemed Dennis Gartman of the Gartman Letter, who sums up this belief perfectly with this story:

"I'm good at trading and I'm wrong a lot according to my wife. When we got married, we sat down the first year and she said you know this is really very sad. You had a good year at trading. You made us a very nice living this year but Dennis you were wrong 53% of the time this year. I thought this was terribly harsh. You couldn't even beat a coin toss. I got out of it by saying, Sweetheart I'm so in love with you that it's colored my ability to think. She bought it. I got another year. We sat down the second year. She said, my wife the accountant, one plus two equals three. She said this is really very sad. You made more money trading this year then you made the previous year. But this year you were wrong 57% of the time. And people pay you for your ideas. And I'm standing by the notion last year that I told you. You can't even beat a coin toss. You need to do better. Sweetheart I'm trying. Third year we sat down. My wife, the accountant, one plus two equals three. She said this is sad. You made more money than you made the previous two years. That's lovely. I want to stay with you. But Dennis, you were wrong 68% of the time this year. Almost 7 out of 10 of your trades lost money. You have got to do better. I told her Laura I'm trying. I'm gonna try. Fourth year we sat down. My wife, the accountant, one plus two equals three. She said, you know, I get it now. You had the best year you ever had. Made more money this year then you made the previous three years. That's lovely. This year you were wrong 81% of the time. I think if you can just be wrong 95% of the time. We're gonna get stinkin' rich. I think I can do it. I think I have it in my grasp to be wrong."

TOP TRADERS BELIEVE IN DEVELOPING A MENTAL MODEL OF THE MARKET

Successful traders develop a story about the market and how it works.

They organize their thinking into a detailed set of beliefs about what works and what does not work in the markets and have a routine in place to monitor its elements.

TOP TRADERS BELIEVE THEY COULD BE WRONG AND ARE WILLING TO ADAPT

Top traders have several beliefs about how the market works, but there will be occasions when those beliefs don't mesh with reality. Even if the belief is logically correct, and all factors line up, the market may do something different. This could be because a big order hits the market or because the trader has missed something important or for plenty of other reasons.

If you hold on too tightly to your beliefs, then you may not see what actually is happening right in front of you and could miss out on significant opportunities or not close a trade when you should. Treat your beliefs with a grain of salt, and be willing to adapt.

TOP TRADERS BELIEVE THAT TRADING IS A SERIOUS BUSINESS, NOT A HOBBY

Successful traders manage their trading as they would a business.

They have a carefully constructed business plan for their trading and follow a "rules-based" approach to selecting, entering, and exiting positions.

A business plan is a formalization of many (if not all) the beliefs in this lesson. It includes:

- Objectives
- Psychology
- Trading strategies
- Contingency plans.

Developing your plan should be a fun experience—and your plan should be enjoyable to read. You're not in school or at work, so make it lively and motivating!

TOP TRADERS BELIEVE IN RECORDING THEIR TRADES DILIGENTLY

If I were to ask you, "What percentage of successful traders record their trades?" what would you say?

- 0%
- 20%
- 50%
- 100%

If you said 100%, you would be the closest to being correct. If I asked you, "What percentage of amateur traders record their trades?" the numbers would be nearly reversed.

Now, what if I ask you, "Are you recording your trades?"

Successful traders have developed the habit of recording each trade they make. They know that without recording their results, they won't know what is working and what is not, so they won't know what to change to improve.

TOP TRADERS BELIEVE IN REVIEWING AND MONITORING THEIR TRADING SYSTEMS

Successful traders will periodically review their strategies, as well as monitor their performance in real time. If a strategy starts to deteriorate, they know about it and can stop trading or switch to a new strategy.

TOP TRADERS BELIEVE THEY ARE THE DETERMINING FACTOR IN THEIR SUCCESS AND BELIEVE IN THE IMPORTANCE OF SELF WORK

"An investment in knowledge pays the best interest."

~ Benjamin Franklin

Top traders know they are the most important factor in the profit equation. Their success or failure is entirely dependent on their skills and abilities, so they spend less time focusing on the market and more time on themselves.

To emulate their success, you want to cultivate a habit of self-improvement that allows you to consistently function at a high level. Occasionally, you will get your butt kicked by the markets. Self-work will give you a foundation of strength to remain persistent even in times of stress.

TOP TRADERS BELIEVE IN PREPARING THEIR MIND BEFORE THEY TRADE (LIKE AN ELITE ATHLETE BEFORE AN EVENT)

Like an elite athlete, successful traders only place trades when they are in an optimal mindset. If they are not mentally on their game, then mistakes happen, and they fail to perform under pressure.

Similar to their athletic counterparts, these traders have a routine to ensure that trading decisions are made when they are in the zone. This could include:

- Visualizing and rehearsing prior to the event (trade)
- Meditating to calm the mind and boost creativity
- Regulating their emotions by using a technique such as "feelings release"
- Working in a trading team

By freeing yourself of negative emotions such as fear or greed, you put yourself in a state from which you can make clear trading decisions.

TOP TRADERS BELIEVE IN TAKING CARE OF BOTH THE BODY AND MIND

There is a deep connection between the performance of the mind and the health of the body. You may notice that when you feel an emotion, you actually feel it in your body. You feel tense across the chest or nervous in the pit of your stomach.

By helping your body relax, you help the mind to relax, too. Successful traders know this and make a conscious effort to maintain their physical health. It's not at all uncommon for top traders to practice yoga or run marathons.

TOP TRADERS BELIEVE IN HAVING A LIFE OUTSIDE OF THE MARKETS

As tempting as it may be to stay continuously attached to the markets, top traders know that sometimes they need to switch off and unplug. If you:

- Have just suffered a loss that was large or traumatic
- Are feeling burnt out
- Are gambling instead of trading because you need some excitement
- Have loved ones who are not getting the attention they need

Then it could be time to take a break. Be proactive about it by planning breaks ahead of time. You have other areas of your life that need attention, too.

TOP TRADERS BELIEVE IN HAVING GRATITUDE

If you have the ability to achieve your goals through trading, you are fortunate. Be thankful, and acknowledge the good things you have in life. Gratitude keeps you happy and helps you to stay grounded when you are successful. Overconfidence and arrogance are the demons that gratitude keeps in check.

TOP TRADERS BELIEVE TRADING IS A GAME, AND THEY MAKE THE RULES

As an individual, you trade in an unlimited environment. No one is telling you what to do. No schoolteacher. No boss. No Forex broker. Successful traders know they make the rules.

Yes, you operate within a framework—a matrix—but within that you are free to choose how you play the game of Forex. So why not choose rules that are advantageous to you?

Each of these beliefs on their own should change the way you think about the markets. Together, they make you elite. Like Neo in *The Matrix*, you might take time to master these beliefs, but when it comes to being a trader, time is one thing you do have. You might spend six months learning these skills and then have twenty or even fifty years of your Forex trading career to benefit from them.

HOW TO DO THEY COMPARE WITH YOUR BELIEFS

In the first chapter of this book, you cataloged some of the beliefs you hold about Forex trading.

How does the list you made compare to the list above?

How many of the beliefs of top traders do you have on your list?

If your list is similar to theirs, that is great. Well done. If not, that's okay, too. By the end of this book, many of those beliefs should be integrated into your trading approach. Before we move on to the next chapter, take a moment to consciously decide which of your old beliefs you would like to keep and which of the beliefs of top traders you are ready to adopt now.

THE SCIENTIFIC PATH TO FINANCIAL FREEDOM THROUGH FOREX TRADING

"Life starts out in the neutral position between profits and losses—it neither fears losses nor desires profits. Life just is, and that's represented by the Grail. However, as a human being develops self-awareness, fear and greed also arise. But when you get rid of the greed (and the fear that comes from lacking), you reach a special unity with all. And that's where great traders and investors emerge."

~ *Van Tharp*

Financial freedom may be closer than you think.

By following these three potentially life-changing steps, you could achieve financial freedom years earlier than you thought you could, or, in some cases, find you are already there:

- Discover your financial freedom number.
- Re-define what financial freedom means to you.
- Set meaningful goals.

This approach to financial freedom is scientific. I want to give you a method that generates action steps specific to your own circumstances.

As with most things that involve human emotion, science will only take you so far. While you will become very clear on what you need to do to achieve financial freedom, you will need to think hard about what is important to you and your loved ones, as well as how much you are prepared to give to achieve your goals.

The human element is what makes goal setting so inspiring and empowering.

GOAL SETTING IS ESSENTIAL TO DEVELOPING A WINNING FOREX TRADING SYSTEM THAT SUITS YOU

"To be a money master, you must be a self-master."

~ *J. P. Morgan*

Before we get into the nuts and bolts of financial freedom, it's important to understand why goal setting is a core element of developing your Forex trading system.

WHAT IS A FOREX TRADING SYSTEM?

A Forex trading system is a set of rules you have for placing a currency trade. For example, the Forex trading systems I use has rules for:

- Objectives

- Defining the market type

- Trade set-ups

- Stalking an entry

- Managing the position once entered (complex exits, scaling, re-entries)

- How much to buy—position-sizing

- When to stop trading the strategy.

The first part of developing a top- quality Forex trading system is defining objectives. For example, here is a set of objectives for an imaginary system.

- I would like my system to make 10% a month;

- I am prepared to risk 2% of my capital to make 10% a month; and

- I only want a 30% chance of losing 2% of my capital.

Once you have defined these objectives, you then develop a set of position-sizing rules that are designed to meet these objectives when you place trades. This is the "how much" element of your investing strategy. For example, this could be:

- I will risk $500 a trade; or

- I will buy 1 lot of EUR/USD.

Without first uncovering your financial freedom number and having a deep understanding of your goals and risk-profile, it's hard to know if these objectives are aligned with your needs.

It's much better to integrate your overall financial goals into your trading system, otherwise, there will be internal conflict—or conflict with a loved one—that will cause mistakes and losses.

In the model of successful trading that I teach in this book, effective goal setting is an essential part of developing objectives for individual trading systems.

THE DEFINITION OF FINANCIAL FREEDOM

"To trade successfully, you need to explore your relationship with money and why you do or do not have enough to trade with."

~ Van Tharp

So what exactly is financial freedom?

One definition states: Financial freedom is having passive income that covers your expenses.

According to this definition, if you are earning more money each month from your trading income than you spend on your lifestyle, then you are technically financially free. Let's take a look at some simple math to see how achievable this is. Note, this example involves making some assumptions and doesn't include taxes.

Say you set a reasonable goal of becoming financially free in ten years' time. You start off with $50,000 in capital and are able to save $100 a week. Over ten years, you are able to earn 15% on average returns.

After following this approach for ten years, you would have $323,694.12. Assuming a 15% return on this capital, you are earning $48,554.12 per year in passive income, or about $4000 a month. If your expenses are less than $4000 a month, you will have achieved financial freedom.

YOUR FINANCIAL FREEDOM NUMBER

To calculate your financial freedom number, figure out your monthly expenses. This is your financial freedom number. For example, if your monthly expenses come to $5339, then your financial freedom number is $5339.

As in the above example, once you have more passive income than you do expenses, you are financially free. Simple. Next, calculate your net worth. You can now work out what return you need on your net worth to achieve financial freedom.

Say your expenses are $100,000 a year, and you have one million dollars. If you could make 10% per year on your one million dollars, you are financially free. If, instead, you have $500,000 but were confident you could make 20% per year, you would also be financially free.

Some of you may be having an "A-ha" moment, as you've realized how close you actually are to what you thought was an elusive goal.

CHANGE YOUR DEFINITION, CHANGE YOUR WORLD

By re-defining what financial freedom means to you, you take one more step beyond the matrix, and start to create a future you own, rather than automatically living a life run by others.

There are numerous paths to financial freedom. Once you open your mind's eye and think creatively, you will realize that, in many ways, you are more limited by your imagination and your willingness to live a life less ordinary than you are by money.

WHAT REALLY IS PASSIVE INCOME?

Possibly the simplest way to re-define the definition of financial freedom is to change what the term "passive income" means to you. Perhaps you choose the belief that you are financially free if, in a twenty-hour workweek, you can generate more money than you need to exceed your financial freedom number.

Or perhaps you would consider yourself financially free if you only needed to work twenty hours a week trading Forex and could take a three-month vacation each year.

Have a deep think about the lifestyle you want to live when you are financially free. You may well not want to stop work altogether. Or maybe you do. Either way is fine. Just make it personal, and above all, realize your goals are very achievable!

QUIT YOUR DAY JOB, MOVE TO A TROPICAL PARADISE, AND LIVE THE DREAM

You should seriously consider it. I mean, why not?

By benefiting from a strong "Western" currency, you can have a lifestyle that would be the envy of most of your friends and family just by moving to the Philippines, Paraguay, or any other stable emerging market.

Okay, while the above is all true, quitting your job and moving your family to a different country is not necessarily that simple (though it can be...where there is a will!). The point of this is to think creatively about how you can redefine your concept of financial freedom. Let your mind wander down all the exciting paths you can come up with, and see what arises. You may be surprised about what you realize you can do. Tropical island, ahoy!

Have fun with this. Think about how you can influence your financial freedom number for the better, or what you could do to change your lifestyle.

(In case you're wondering, we actually did do this. When I started my Forex business, my wife and I quit our jobs and moved to Phuket in Thailand, then to New Zealand, and on to Singapore).

SETTING MEANINGFUL GOALS

Once you have uncovered your current financial freedom number and realized you can re-define financial freedom to suit your needs, it's important to start thinking about what you truly want from life.

Having enough money to cover your expenses is great. But if you can link your trading to a higher purpose, you raise yourself to yet another level. Start by asking yourself this question:

If I achieve my Forex trading goals, what will it enable me to do?

Now get out a pen and paper, and spend five to fifteen minutes, brainstorming potential answers. This could be anything from "put my children through university" to "retire in five years and live off the income."

Next, you want you to take a moment to think about these questions:

What would you do to achieve that goal? What would you give? And how committed are you to making sure it happens?"

When I have asked people this question in the past, the main answer I get is, "Anything, anything, whatever it takes."

When you do this process, be sure to include your family. If you set objectives on your own without input from your loved ones, you could create conflict that could impact your trading performance.

It's best to talk openly and honestly, without an agenda. When you listen carefully and non-judgmentally to the concerns of others, you are sure to come to an even better solution. If you are having trouble in this area, try reading Stephen Covey's *Third Alternative*.

By the way, "I want to make money" is not a good goal. It's not specific or emotive enough to really work. It's best to come up with a number (like your financial freedom number) and very personal reasons why you want to achieve your goals.

Studies show that if you set specific and meaningful goals, you are far more likely to achieve success.

GOALS ARE A WORK IN PROGRESS

"No plan survives first contact with the enemy"

~ Military adage

Are you a perfectionist? I certainly can be. These perfectionist tendencies can stop us from getting started. Rather it is better to set goals, identify the first step you need to take to achieve the goal and then get stuck right in. The key is commitment to working toward a goal that challenges you.

When you set goals, realize they don't have to be carved in stone, and every step does not need to be mapped out. Your initial goals are likely to change down the track. Keep them simple, robust, and flexible.

Good goals have many avenues to success. If you only have one way to achieve your goal, you severely reduce the likelihood of making it.

To use a non-trading example, if your goal is to marry a specific person, and that person is already taken or does not like you, then you are stuck. But if you have a goal to marry a caring, attractive person who loves you to bits, then you have options!

A TEN-FOLD RETURN

Every moment you spend working on your goals will pay bountiful dividends down the track. Your investment of time now will be returned ten or a hundred or more times over.

By obtaining extreme clarity about what you want out of life, not only do you create a roadmap to achieve your goals, you will have lit a fire within. The burning passion that goals inspire helps you to stay disciplined, avoid procrastination, and keep pushing through fatigue or hardship.

Goal setting works on a subconscious level. Aside from the conscious actions you will take, your subconscious mind is now hard at work, finding ways for you to achieve your goals. You have awakened the sleeping giant within, and it will relentlessly work on your behalf to guide you toward financial success.

CHOOSE YOURSELF

Take the time now to think very carefully about what you want out of life.

Spend some time sitting on a park bench, walking around the block or visiting a café with a loved one, and brainstorm about your future. Take detailed notes, and make sure you enjoy the process. If you feel bad at all, sit back, take a deep breath, and just be in the moment. And when you are ready again, let the creativity flow.

The more time you spend on this exercise, the better. So don't rush it. You will know when you have found the goal that motivates and excites you the most.

Craft a Compelling Model of the Market

"Our decision making process is to determine the criteria by which we make decisions in the market. Those criteria—I call them principles—we systematized. These principles determine what we do under different circumstances. In other words, we make decisions about the criteria we use to make decisions. We don't make decisions about individual positions."

~ Ray Dalio

To step outside the matrix, you need to be aware of where its boundaries lie. In the first two chapters of this book, you learned about your beliefs and how different they are from the beliefs of top Forex traders. In the third chapter, you took a scientific approach to goal setting by uncovering your financial freedom number and redefining what financial freedom means to you.

In this chapter, you'll continue your journey down the trading rabbit hole by creating a model of the Forex market that you will use in a future chapter to develop your true edge as a trader.

When you know how the market's wheels turn, you can direct your activities to the areas you enjoy and in which you can spot opportunity. This is different from the majority of traders who blindly trade strategies or indicators without any sort of guiding framework.

What Is a Compelling Model of the Market?

A compelling model of the market is a framework around what makes the market tick. It's an overview of what's going on, what works, and what doesn't, along with how to implement trades in a way that provides the best trading opportunity.

A good market model typically includes both fundamental and technical (price) information about the Forex market. For example, you might consider how the following things impact currency markets when you develop models:

- Central banks and interest rates

- Support and resistance areas

- News announcements

- Geopolitics

- Supply and demand

- Chart patterns

- Dealing ranges

- How currency prices move (who moves the markets).

- Where opportunities lie (and why).

- Which strategies work and which don't.

- Correlations between currencies and other asset classes.

With this type of information you can start to make good, organized decisions that give you an edge over other market participants.

YOUR MARKET MODEL'S PURPOSE

"We test our criteria to make sure they are timeless and universal...this broad analysis through time and geography gives us a unique perspective relative to other managers. For example, to understand the current U.S zero interest rate, deleveraging environment, we need to understand what happened a long time ago, such as the 1930's and in other countries such as Japan in the post bubble era."

~ Ray Dalio

When you are developing a model of the market, you will want to keep in mind the reasons you need to have this model in place. The goal of having a model of the market is not about being "knowledgeable"; it's about being practical. You are looking to gain three things from your model:

1. Information to guide you on what to trade.

2. Information to guide you on how to trade.

3. Information that will protect you from losses.

Some traders become so obsessed with being "right" or showing off their knowledge that they lose sight of what is important. They tend to have a big ego, and this does not make them good traders in the long run.

TRADE WHAT IS IN FRONT OF YOU

"A great Soros Quote is, 'invest first; investigate later'. You don't want to get fixated on needing a nice story for the trade."

~ Colm O'Shea

It is all well and good to have a compelling model of the market, but it is important to realize it is there to serve you. If, for example, you have a view that sees risk everywhere, and that causes you to stay out of a good trade, then your model is not serving you well.

Your model could even be right, but if the market does not agree, then you could be left out on a limb. Highly successful traders have a compelling model of the market, but at the same time, they are comfortable with the model being wrong. What's important is what is going on in front of them.

THE PIECES OF THE PUZZLE

"The biggest public fallacy is that the market is always right. The market is nearly always wrong. I can assure you of that."

~ James B. Rogers, Jr.

The Forex trading landscape is like a giant jigsaw puzzle—where all the parts don't match. It's not "one size fits all", either. A top trader has a model that is developed to fit their own personality and style. Despite this uniqueness, there are common elements. You can craft your compelling model of the market by asking the following questions.

Afterward, I will provide some resources to help you with the answers.

- How does the financial system work?

- How do central banks influence markets?

- What will be the impact of any government or regulatory changes?

- How is the current global debt situation likely to impact your trading?

- What market type are we in currently (bull or bear)?

- What trading strategies are likely to work in the current environment?

- Do you believe in news trading (and why or why not)?

- Do you believe in fundamental information? If so, how would you use such information in your trading?

- How does order flow impact currency movements?

- Do you believe in scalping (and why or why not)?

- Do you believe in technical analysis of chart patterns (and why or why not)? If yes, what specific areas are of interest?

- Are there any particular "schools" of trading that you believe in, such as Fibonacci theory, (and why or why not)?

- Do dealers hunt stops, and if they do, why?

- How does the "big money" trade Forex?

- Do you believe in taking a contrarian approach and trading reversals?

- Do you believe in trend following?

- How do correlations impact currency movements?

- How do equity markets and commodities impact currency movements?

- How are major currency pairs different from cross-rates and exotics?

- How does the commitment of traders in the currency futures market impact the spot rates?

- Where do you see opportunity?

- What trends exist right now?

- What risks do you see?

- What are your specific skills or edges?

- What are your areas of interest?

- What would you like to become an expert in?

- What are you trading in right now and why?

- What demographic trends do you see?

- What is your view of inflation? What about deflation?

- How do you think the gold and silver markets work?

- How will you monitor your model of the market?

- How will you avoid bias and data-mining problems?

- How and when will you revise your model?

- Enough work for you?

The good news is there is no requirement to go into detail on these just yet. Your market model will be a work in progress that you continually add to over your Forex trading career.

For now, I want you to pick two questions—whichever two most interest you—from the above list to answer, and I am going to give you three more.

1. What trading strategies are likely to work in the current environment?

2. What are your specific skills or edges?

3. What are your areas of interest?

4. You choose

5. You choose

Once you have answered these five questions, your model of the Forex trading market will be sufficient to start formulating a comprehensive and winning Forex trading plan.

As a side note, it's important not to get overwhelmed by this task and to keep it simple. If you only want to answer the first three questions, that is okay. Then later you can come back and review the model or add to it over time.

RESOURCES FOR CRAFTING YOUR MARKET MODEL

On the resources page on my website, I keep an up-to-date list of resources to help you build a market model. You can access it here: **www.fxrenew.com/forex-resources**

A BLUEPRINT FOR SUCCESS

"There are three things you need to make money in a market. You need a decent fundamental story, a good trend that looks like it will carry on, and the market handling news the way you think it should. Bull markets ignore any bad news, and any good news is a reason for a further rally."

~ Michael Platt

As you answer the model-of-the-market questions above, you will notice that you start to have trading insights. You will see how you can use logic and intuition to choose to trade in a manner that simply makes sense. You will start to understand how and where to trade and notice areas of risk to avoid.

While it may be tempting to dive deeply into this foundational information, you don't need to do it all at once. Follow the KISS (Keep it Simple Stupid) principle, and do only what's necessary. Information overload is not going to help at this point.

You can see from the above quote by Michael Platt how he has distilled his market model into a succinct and simple trading approach. This really is your objective, so don't get carried away.

In addition, you should not feel the need to read or watch the financial news every minute of the day—in fact, you will be well served to turn it *off*. Instead, focus on developing your own knowledge of how the market works.

For now, I leave you with a basic task. Get out your notepad and answer the five questions asked of you above. It won't take you long, and the benefit will be large.

How to Get an Edge and Trade Like the "House" at a Casino

"It does not matter if you win or lose on any given trade, as long as you get the process correct."

~ Scott Ramsey

Imagine you owned a casino. Every day, thousands of bets are made, some of which you—as the house—will naturally lose. But at the end of the day, you are always in profit, and sometimes, spectacularly so. This happens because you have a built-in edge. Each game played by the punter who walks in the door has been carefully designed so that over a long enough timeframe, the house will always win.

In this chapter, we will look at how you can become the "house" when you are trading Forex by developing an edge over the markets. This requires an understanding of some basic concepts around statistics and probability, starting with the true role of entries and exits.

The True Role of Entries and Exits

"Having the faith to stick with the system because I knew that I had the edge was something that helped me a great deal when I went into the pit."

~ Blair Hull

To continue with the gambling analogy, each trade is like a draw from a lucky dip. The better your entries and exits, the more winners in the draw, the easier it will be for your trading strategy to meet your objectives.

Your job as a trader when it comes to entries and exits, is to add as many winning tickets into the draw as possible—or to add in tickets that win a much bigger amount than the cost of the ticket. This is what the house does at the casino. They stack the draw in their favor, so that over the long term, they are guaranteed to win.

When you grasp this concept, you will realize how entries and exits fit into the bigger picture of your trading strategy, and they will lose some of their mystical qualities appeal. You don't need to have a strategy that is perfect, just one that produces enough winners over time, so that with the right position-sizing model (more on this soon), you can achieve your objectives.

OBJECTIVES COME FIRST

"What really matters is the long-run distribution of outcomes from your trading techniques, systems, and procedures."

~ William Eckhart

Building a trading strategy is a little like building a house. When you construct a house, you decide how many rooms it will have, the layout, how many floors, and so on. These decisions are based on your needs (objectives), budget (investing capital), and what suits your personality (psychology). Similarly, when you develop a trading system, you get to choose things like the risk/reward ratio, win rate, and the number of trades you will take, i.e. you want to place one trade a day. More on this in the next chapter.

This may come as a surprise to some traders whose approach has typically been to back-test a situation to see if it has an edge, then look to trade every time that situation occurs. For example, they may test what happens every time the 50-period moving average crosses the 100-period moving average. Then, if they believe that type of trade has an edge, they will place a trade every time the moving averages cross. This may be a good way for a well-capitalized system trader to go about their business, but as a discretionary trader, it is not so helpful.

A better approach for a discretionary trader is to choose the objective first, and then you develop a set of rules and processes to achieve those objectives. This is what happens in the hedge fund industry, where a fund might look to achieve a 20% return with no greater than a 7% per annum drawdown a year. The hedge fund trader will know the objectives of the fund (typically, this is the type of risk-adjusted return investors are after), and then they will design an approach that achieves those returns.

ARE HIGH PROBABILITY ENTRIES BETTER?

When developing a trading strategy, it's important to understand that on the surface, probabilities may not be what they seem. To the less-experienced trader, a high win rate may be seen as desirable. After all, wouldn't it be great if 90% of the trades you placed were winners?

To explore this concept further, let's take a look at these three examples of trading strategies.

- Strategy 1

    Strategy 1 generates 10 trades a month with a 90% win rate. Winning trades make $100, and losing trades lose $1000.

- Strategy 2

    Strategy 2 generates 80 trades a month with a 60% win rate. Winning trades make $60, and losing trades lose $50.

- Strategy 3

    Strategy 3 generates 10 trades a month with a 15% win rate. Winning trades make $1800, and losing trades lose $150.

Before you read on, which trading strategy would you prefer? Note it down, along with the reasons you chose this strategy.

Here are the results for a month's trading for each strategy in dollars:

- Strategy 1 with a 90% win rate had a $100 loss
- Strategy 2 with a 60% win rate had a $1280 profit
- Strategy 3 with a 15% win rate had a $1425 profit.

What do you notice here?

The strategy that made the most profit had the lowest winning rate—and the strategy that lost money had the highest win rate. Now, would you still choose the same trading strategy you chose above?

When you are developing your entry and exit, the one with the most wins is not always the best. Be careful not to fall into this trap. What you are after is the one that give you the biggest edge, or in statistical terms, a "positive expectancy".

WHAT IS POSITIVE EXPECTANCY?

"The expectancy is really the amount you'll make on the average per dollar risked. If you have a methodology that makes you 50 cents or better per dollar risked, that's superb. Most people don't."

~ Van Tharp

Note that the work below on expectancy and "R-multiples" is based on the original work of Van Tharp and is repeated here with his permission.

Expectancy is how much on average you are likely to make or lose when you place a trade in terms of your risk/reward ratio. An expectancy above zero means you have positive outcome.

For example, if you make on average $1.20 for every dollar you risk, then your expectation of profit would be 1.2 times your risk. In this case, you have an expectancy of 0.2 (positive). If you make .80 for every dollar you risk, then your profit would be 0.8 times your risk. In the second case, your expectancy would be -0.2 (negative).

You calculate your expectancy of your entire trading strategy by averaging the risk/reward over a series of trades, but before we get to the equation, it helps to understand what Tharp calls "R-multiples".

R Multiples, an Introduction to Defining Your Initial Risk

"One of the real secrets of trading success is to think in terms of risk-to-reward ratios every time you take a trade."

~ Van Tharp

R-multiples are a way of defining the initial risk you take on a trade by thinking in terms of risk/reward.

If you place a trade with a stop-loss 50 pips away from the market, and you are buying a standard lot, then your loss would be (roughly) $500 if the trade went against you. This initial loss of $500 or 50 pips is your 1R risk. The R, of course, stands for risk.

You can express your trades in terms of R, instead of in terms of dollar. For example, if you place a trade that risks $100, and you make $200, you have made 2R (two times your risk). If you lose the $100 you would have lost 1R.

If you talk to a trader who uses R-multiples risking $1000 per trade and making $2400 in a week, they may say, "I made 2.4R this week."

How to Calculate the Expectancy of Your Trading Strategy

Now that you know what an R-multiple is, we can get back to calculating your expectancy. I know you may not have a system just yet, but don't worry; just keep this formula in mind as something to come back to down the track.

To calculate your expectancy, first, you add up the total R-value of your Forex trades, and then you divide this total by the number of trades you have made.

Here is the formula:

(total R) / (number of trades) = expectancy

For example:

If you had placed 30 trades and earned 45R in the process, your equation would look like this:

45R /30 = 1.5

In this case, your system has an expectancy of 1.5R (which is very good).

POSITION-SIZING RULES ARE DEVELOPED INDEPENDENT OF YOUR ENTRIES AND EXITS

Part of the value of thinking about your trades in terms of expectancy is that it separates your success into two distinct components, each of which can be worked on independently.

- An entry and exit strategy that generates an average number of R-multiples over time; and

- A position-sizing algorithm that is then applied on top of the entry and exit strategy.

Essentially, you have a set of rules for when to enter and exit the market, and then you have rules for "how much to trade".

The performance of your trading strategy as a whole will depend on the combined performance of both these elements, minus any trading mistakes you make.

To return again to the casino analogy, while a casino has an edge, if they get a high roller in town, and they accept a bet that is too big for their bank and lose, then they could get themselves into serious trouble. This would be an example of them making a mistake with their position-sizing model.

Now you know what an edge is, let's look at some ways to get one.

Ways to Get an Edge

"One very interesting thing I've found is that virtually every successful trader I know ultimately ended up with a trading style suited to his personality."

~ Randy McKay

We can't all buy a casino and rig the odds in our favor, but luckily, in the Forex market, we don't have to. Market behavior is irrational, so often situations arise where there are opportunities to place trades at prices that provide you with a significant advantage if you can learn to spot them.

Don't forget that your edge on entry is only part of the equation. How much you actually make at the end of the day will be dictated by your exits and how much you trade (position sizing), as well. Importantly, edges can be combined, and it is often better to have more than one thing going for you when you trade. Just don't over complicate things.

In later chapters, we go into detail about how to add each of these edges into your trading plan. For now, let's take a brief look at some of the edges available for Forex traders.

Global Macro

Global macro is the big picture of supply and demand factors and geopolitical events that impact financial markets. Examples of global macro traders are George Soros, who is famous for "breaking the bank of England", or Market Wizard Louis Bacon, whose hedge fund returned an average of 35% a year for investors for more than a decade.

In your compelling model of the market from chapter 4, you will have started to build a framework that includes global macro elements. In the context of edges, you use global macro analysis to place trades in the currency market around these ideas.

NEWS EVENTS

Traders can look trading opportunities within the news events that are released throughout the week. For example, you may take the outcome of high-impact data releases, such as non-farm payroll or central bank rate announcement.

Upcoming news events can be found by perusing the week-ahead data or by reading reports from trusted sources. Ideally, you want to know what is coming up for the currency pairs you are trading, and understand the potential impact of these events on your positions.

TECHNICAL ANALYSIS

Technical analysis uses price patterns on charts to determine future price movements. The basic premise behind technical analysis is that these patterns represent market psychology, and people tend to do the same thing over and over again, so when you spot one, it gives you an insight into what is going to happen next. In particular, technical analysis can help with:

- Identifying the market type so you only trade with the trend
- Finding low-risk, high reward entries
- Buying with momentum
- Where to place your stop-loss
- What your profit objective for the trade should be
- How to manage the position after you have entered.

There are several schools of technical analysis, be it simple price action, Elliot wave and Gann theory, or technical indicators. I will teach you some methods later in the book.

Forex Trading Signals and Ideas

Forex trading signals provide a handy edge. You get to keep control of your position sizing and your objectives (which are the things that actually make you money), and you get access to trades that help you to time your entries and exits.

You are alerted to ideas that you might not find yourself or that confirm your trades. It's much better to trade as part of a team rather than on your own.

FX Renews signal providers are ex-bank traders who have significant experience providing signals, not only to retail traders, but also to an exclusive clientele of around forty major banks and hedge funds.

You can get a free trial of the Forex trading signals here.

www.fxrenew.com/forex-signals

Other Edges

There are hundreds of potential ways to gain an edge over the market. The one you choose needs to suit you, specifically. It's hard to borrow someone's edge, exactly, though it is easy to borrow one and modify it slightly to suit you. Keep an open mind, and be on the lookout for methods of Forex trading that suit you.

Here are some you can consider:

- Correlation Studies

  It is worth taking note of the correlation between different currency pairs and markets. For example, the moves on gold, bonds, or the equities could impact currency pairs and vice versa.

- Flow Information

  Understanding where large orders are sitting in the market and what large orders are in play is a significant edge if you can access this information.

- Trend Following

"Trend following is an exercise in observing and responding to the ever-present moment of now."

~ Ed Seykota

Originally made popular by famous trend followers "the Turtles"*, trend followers often use computer-driven trading models designed to capture large moves.

*Named after a vat growing turtles in Singapore, the Turtles are a group of futures traders hired by Market Wizards Richard Dennis and William Eckhart to solve the question, "Are traders born with it, or can trading be taught?"

- Counter-Trend/ Reversion to The Mean

Some traders look for statistical anomalies on the price, such as the price moving several standard deviations from the mean, as opportunities to profit.

- Specialization

Some traders choose the path of specialization. They have a particular interest or skill in one currency pair. A trader may choose to be an expert in only the NZD/USD, for example, and get to know everything about that currency pair.

BE CAREFUL YOUR ENTRY AND EXIT ARE NOT YOUR ONLY (OR MOST IMPORTANT) SOURCE OF EDGES

It's easy to get sucked in by the mysticism of technical analysis and the like, and these methods can provide you with a statistical edge (more winning draws). The "glamorous" nature of entries as perpetuated by Forex educators out to make a buck means traders focus far too much time on when to enter a trade and not enough on other aspects of their trading plan that are of equal, if not greater, importance.

Each chapter in this book is designed to provide you with an advantage. For example, by having clear objectives and developing a compelling model of the market, you have edges over those who don't.

Additionally, as a small trader, you have some very clear advantages over your larger, institutional brethren. Let's take a look at some of these now.

NOT HAVING TO TRADE

As a small trader with only yourself to answer to, you are never required to place a trade. On the contrary, institutional traders are often forced to take a position. In the inter-bank market, their job is often to have a position in the market—they have zero choice. You, on the other hand, can wait patiently for the right time to enter, and stay out of the market altogether if you don't know what is going on. While institutional traders may have more time and resources than you do, this edge is very significant.

BEING AGILE WITH YOUR POSITION SIZING

"Individual investors may feel they are at a disadvantage to large hedge fund managers, but they actually have an important advantage: Their small trading size allows them to move in and out of positions...with virtually no market impact."

~ Jack Schwager, Author of the Market Wizards books, discussing insights from Kevin Daly

As a small trader you can be very flexible in the sizes you trade compared to institutional money. You can place stop-losses, and when you wish to close positions, you won't tend to move the market. Institutional Forex traders don't have these luxuries; their larger positions can move the market, and liquidity can dry up, leaving them with a worse price. Often bank traders are forced to work very large positions of hundreds of millions of currency units, as they have a corporate order to fill.

HAVING THE FREEDOM TO TRADE ANY CURRENCY YOU CHOOSE

As an individual, you can choose to trade the currency pairs that are going to give you the best chance of achieving your goals. Imagine how big an advantage this gives you over a money manager who can only trade in one currency, for example.

LAY DOWN YOUR CHIPS...AS THE HOUSE

"Trading is a matter of probabilities. Any trading strategy, no matter how effective, will be wrong a certain percentage of time. Traders often confuse concepts of winning and losing trades with good and bad trades. A good trade can lose money, and a bad trade can win money."

~ Jack Schwager, Author of the Market Wizards books, discussing his learnings from Tom Claugus.

It's time to turn the tables. Instead of being the chump who comes to the market and is guaranteed to lose, you can start to become the "house" who is guaranteed to win. Your first step in this process is simply to read about the statistical concepts in this lesson until you feel you have a handle on them. They are an important part of your departure from the trading matrix.

Please—and I can't stress this enough—don't get sidetracked by the excitement of market analysis and neglect the other aspects of your trading plan. So many traders (me, included, at one time) get enamored by back-testing combinations of indicators on charts and ignore the more important areas, such as objectives, psychology, and building good processes. Keep working though this book step-by-step, and you will find you allocate the right amount of time to each area.

How to Set Forex Trading Objectives That Keep Your Risk Small and Let You Win Big

"The only thing that disturbs me is poor money management."

~ Bruce Kovner

It's far too easy to take this Forex thing casually. You can open an account with a broker in the blink of an eyelid, and in two more blinks, you can be trading Forex. But Forex is a game of skill, played by some of the most sophisticated, intelligent, well-connected men and women in the world. Every time you trade, it's like playing chess against a chess master (not to burst anyone's bubble!). So do you think that having sloppy objectives for what you are trying to achieve is going to cut it?

Nope...you are right—they sure won't.

The good thing is that once you do understand how to craft proper objectives, a number of nice things happen:

- You stop losing money (even if you don't always make any)
- You stop over-trading
- You trade with a much greater sense of purpose and control
- You improve your discipline
- You start to hold on to your positions instead of cutting your winners short

Objectives are the first and most crucial step in system development and where we now shift our focus.

YOUR TRADING PLAN TEMPLATE

Your trading plan template is a carefully crafted document you can fill out as you go through this next section of this book.

If you have not downloaded it already, you can get it when you subscribe to my free course.

www.fxrenew.com/forex-course

FROM FOUNDATION TO SYSTEM DEVELOPMENT

"You have to start with your goal."

~ Ray Dalio

The first chapters in this book have been foundational in nature. Now we move to a more tactical level, where you will develop a simple, robust, and insightful trading system that will eventually meet the financial goals you have been establishing since *The Scientific Path to Financial Freedom through Forex Trading*.

This starts with setting objectives for your system. Every good trading system has very clear and well-defined objectives. In fact, Market Wizard Van Tharp suggests that objectives are so important that up to 50% of system development should be spent on objectives.

The main objectives you will need for your system are:

- Returns
- Maximum drawdown
- Chance of maximum drawdown
- Trading opportunity
- Win Rate
- Targeted risk/reward ratio
- Maximum number of positions

Once you have clarity on these objectives, you will have the ingredients you need to develop a robust position-sizing model, to construct a set of trading rules to achieve your goals, and to trade with discipline.

Constructing a Return Objective

"Two of the cardinal sins of trading—giving too much rope and taking profits prematurely—are both attempts to make current positions more likely to succeed, to the severe detriment of long-term performance."

~ William Eckhardt

Saying, "I want to make lots of money," is *not* a good objective.

Instead, you want to be very specific about how much you want to make and over what time period. For example:

"I want to return 10% on my capital over the course of a month."

If you are not specific in your objectives, you will make mistakes when you trade. In particular, you will cut winning trades short, as you are not clear on what you need to achieve from the trade. How to decide what is right for you? You have several considerations:

- How much capital are you allocating to Forex trading?
- How much time do you have for trading?
- Are you day (short), swing (medium), or position (long-term) trading?
- What size drawdown (the maximum loss on your account) you are willing to accept?
- How many different systems you will be running?
- What are your individual psychological needs?
- What is your current experience and competence level?

Ultimately, the amount you be targeting to make will be personal choices specific to your goals, but here is a rough guide based on your trading style:

- Short-term trading—5-25% return a month

- Medium-term—1.5-10% return a month

- Long-term—10-100% return a year

If you are struggling to come up with a return objective, don't get too stressed. Pick something from the list above that fits. It's your returns in combination with other objectives that matter most of all, and you can always scale up or adapt over time. For now, you just need a starting point.

OBJECTIVES BASED ON YOUR FINANCIAL FREEDOM NUMBER

Your objectives could be based on your financial freedom goals from chapter 3. In particular, it's useful to know your financial freedom number, so you can work back toward your profit objective. For example, if your financial freedom number is $5000 a month, then the objective for your trading system could be to make $5000 a month. If you have $50,000 to trade with, then that would mean your profit objective would be to make a 10% per month return.

FUTURE MONEY MANAGER, OBJECTIVES ARE CRITICAL FOR YOU

For those of you who are one day looking to manage money, objectives are of particular significance. You need to understand what objectives you will be assessed against and then build a system that fits. Here is what a hedge fund head trader I know has to say on the topic:

"The first thing traders looking to manage money should do is gain an understanding of the metrics that they need to achieve, ideally *before* embarking on creating the track record—then devise a risk management/trading strategy that achieves those metrics."

For example, you will want to understand Sharp and Sortino ratios if you are managing money.

STARTING OUT IN FOREX

Not all of you are going to want to start with the full amount of capital you will eventually trade with. That is, of course, okay. Start with an amount you are comfortable with. What is critical is that you trade it as if it is a smaller version of your targeted account. Don't use trading a smaller size as an excuse to take a punt, or you will develop bad habits.

NOTIONAL FUNDING

Notional funding is used when you don't plan to fully fund your trading account. For example, you may fund your account with $10,000, but you trade it as if you have $50,000 in the account. This is a common way to be efficient with your trading capital. If you are using notional funding in your trading account, then you will base your objective off the full amount ($50,000 in the above case).

BALANCING THE EQUATION WITH A MAXIMUM DRAWDOWN OBJECTIVE

"Your job as a trader [is to] protect the direction of the [equity line]."

~ Steve Clark

In order to make money, you need to risk money. But the good thing is that you are in control of what you risk. A drawdown is the amount of loss you are willing to sustain in order to go for your profit objective. For example, if you had a trading account with $10,000 in it, and you lost $1,000, then you would be experiencing a 10% drawdown.

While you might never want to have a drawdown, they cannot be avoided altogether (except by not trading!) and should be seen as simply a cost of doing business. This means you should plan for them, prior to their occurrence. When traders fail to plan for losses, they tend to make mistakes and exit their trades at the wrong time.

How Big a Drawdown Should You Allow?

Drawdowns can be tough. To make it easy on your trading psychology, you want them to be as small as possible, but typically, the bigger the drawdown you are willing to accept, the greater your returns will be.

To use the example from history, the famous "turtles", who were trained by Market Wizards William Eckhart and Richard Dennis, had a combined return of close to 25% per year but at the same time had to suffer through a drawdown of 35% and multiple smaller drawdowns. The turtle traders were mechanical-trend followers who, by nature, experienced large drawdowns. If you are a discretionary Forex trader, you have the ability to do much better than this.

Generally, you will want a maximum drawdown of no greater than 50% of your return objective. For example, if you have a return objective of 10% a month, your maximum risk should be no more than 5% a month. I would suggest you be even more conservative with your drawdowns, and risk no more than 2-3% a month if you are looking to make 10%, or 10% a year if you are looking to make 50%.

Market Wizard Van Tharp said that if he were a short-term trader, he would have the objectives of risking no more than 2% a month in order to make 25%. However, it's important not to constrain yourself from taking the opportunities you have in front of you because of your drawdown limit. For some people, taking a large amount of risk allows them to generate very big profits.

RECOVERING FROM A DRAWDOWN

It's important to note that once you go past a 25% drawdown it can be difficult to recover. As you can see on the following table, if you have a 25% drawdown, you need to make a 33% return on your account to recover. But if you have a 50% drawdown, you will need a 100% return just to recover. Consider the following table:

Loss of capital (%)	Gain to recover (%)
5	5.3
10	11.1
15	17.6
20	25.0
25	33.3
30	42.9
35	53.8
40	66.7
45	81.8
50	100.00
55	122.00
60	150.00

PERCENT CHANCE OF THE DRAWDOWN OBJECTIVE

Once you establish a maximum drawdown objective, you want to consider how comfortable you would be experiencing the drawdown. This will greatly affect your position-sizing model. For example, if you decided that your maximum drawdown is 10%, and you are willing to risk a 100% chance of this happening in order to achieve your goals, then you would trade very differently than if you only wanted a 5% chance of ever experiencing your maximum drawdown.

WHAT TO DO WHEN YOU HAVE A DRAWDOWN

"Managing money is real life, not some bullshit strategist fantasy world."

~ Martin Taylor

If you experience a drawdown, you have a few options, including:

- Reduce your position size.
- Keep trading the same size and wait for the winning trades.
- Pause your trading and review what's working and what's not.
- Stop trading altogether.

You should have it written in your trading plan exactly what to do.

Market Wizard Michael Platt has a policy that if any of his traders hit their drawdown limit of 3% a year (yes, 3% a year—each of his traders are allocated a billion dollars), then he cuts their allocation in half and allows them to risk 3% of the new allocation. If they lose that, then they would be out of a job.

TRADING OPPORTUNITY

How often you trade will significantly impact your position sizing and trading system performance. Don't ignore the importance of being very clear about how often you trade. If you don't maintain strict control over how many trades you are placing, you will likely trade too much, taking poor-quality trades that you got excited about in the heat of the moment but regret in hindsight.

Many traders tend to overtrade, and their returns suffer because of costs and mistakes, such as the failure to hold on to the big winners. Warren Buffett said you only need one good idea a year to get rich over the long-term if you know how to capitalize on it (you capitalize on good ideas with position sizing).

Of course, more active trading systems can be incredibly good at producing consistent returns, as well. The key is planning how many trades you want your system to take, building a position-sizing model around this (see the next chapter), and then being disciplined in only taking the number of trades you are supposed to take.

I look for 1-3 trades a week in order to achieve my objectives. This forces me to filter out the lower-quality opportunities and focus on the best ones. For our signal program at FX Renew, which is a day trading approach, we choose the one best trade for the day from those we have available. This tight control of how often to trade keeps returns smooth.

YOU CAN CHOOSE HOW MANY TRADES YOU GET RIGHT

"Frankly, I don't see markets; I see risks, rewards, and money."

~ Larry Hite

As alluded to in the previous chapter, you get to choose how many trades you get right versus how many you get wrong. This is your win rate. For example, you might have an objective to win 50% of your trades.

The crux of this decision is your trading psychology. If you recall in chapter 5, we used an example of three different trading systems with different win rates. In that example, the system with the worst win rate was the most profitable, as the winning trades were very large. But for many traders, this would have been a very difficult system to operate, as you would have to experience a lot of losers while you wait for the winners, which can lead to mistakes.

In general, the higher your targeted win rate, the lower your profit per trade is going to be. For example, if you want 80% of your trades to be winners, you will generally need to take your profits a lot quicker. Conversely, if you have a targeted win rate of only 20%, by definition, you will need to let your profits run for big wins.

On the flip side of the coin, a very consistent trading system with a high win rate can still work very well. If a high win rate system generates returns with limited drawdowns, it may allow you to trade with a much larger position size, making up for the lack of big winners it produces. It is not that low or high win rates are better, it's just that different approaches are going to produce different outcomes, and you need to be aware of what you are getting yourself into. I prefer to combine the two methods, using a scale-out approach, which we will cover later in this book.

Have a think about what win rate you would like to target. Unless you feel you have excellent entries, I would suggest you go no higher than 65%. And unless you feel you have an iron temperament for handling losses, I would suggest you go no lower than 35%.

WINNING AND LOSING STREAKS

Trading systems go through periods of losing and winning streaks. The lower your targeted win rate, the longer your potential losing streak could be. Conversely, the higher the win rate, the longer the potential winning streak could be.

As mentioned above, neither option is right or wrong. But if you can understand how many losses in a row you are likely to have when trading your system, this will help you remain disciplined. If you expect to have several periods where you have five losses in a row, then you are not going to panic when you have three. It also helps you to understand when something has gone wrong. If your trading strategy has more losses than you expected, it could be a sign that it is not appropriate for the current market conditions, or the edge has broken down.

Risk/Reward Objectives

"Knowing when you're going to exit a trade is the only way to determine how much you're really risking in any given trade or investment. If you don't know when you're getting out, then, in effect, you're risking 100% of your money."

~ Van Tharp

Once you have chosen your win rate percentage, you want to attach a targeted risk/reward ratio to your trade. For example, if you have a targeted win rate of 50%, then you might decide you want your winners to make three times your losses, on average. If you win half the time, but make roughly 300% of your risk when you do win, you can still expect a healthy return. To further clarify, this means that if you were risking a $100 loss if the trade goes against you, then you would want to make $300 per trade if it goes for you.

In theory, the higher your win rate, the lower your risk/reward and vice versa. Imagine if you only wanted to win 10% of the time. You would need to make a lot on your winners! Setting your system's risk/reward profile then becomes a balance between consistency (win rate) and profitability (risk/reward).

In theory, to adjust the risk/reward on your system, you simply widen or tighten the stop-loss. In practice, you want to look for situations that have a superior risk/reward profile. For now, have a think about how you want to trade. Are you the kind of trader who likes to swing for big wins? Or are you the kind of trader who likes to win a lot and take small gains from the market?

Targeted Expectancy

When building a trading system, a savvier trader will have a targeted expectancy they are trying to achieve. The better the expectancy, the easier it will be for the trader to achieve their goals using their position-sizing model.

MAXIMUM NUMBER OF POSITIONS

"One of the first lessons my boss taught me is that price is irrelevant; it is all about controlling the size of your position."

~ Steve Clark

In Forex trading, you have plenty of leverage available on your account, so it is very easy for the inexperienced player to take on more trades than they can handle. In your trading plan, specify a maximum number of positions you can have open at any one time.

How many is too many? This depends on your trading approach. A long-term trend, systematic follower may have up to 20 positions or more open at any one time, whereas a discretionary trader may keep it to 5 or less.

You also need to consider the number of correlated positions you hold at any one time, along with your portfolio heat. More about these later in this book.

INTEGRATING MULTIPLE TRADING SYSTEMS

"Each strategy develops a track record that we deeply understand and then combine in a portfolio of diversified strategies."

~ Ray Dalio

You may find you want to run multiple trading systems at one time. If you do, then you want to set specific objectives for each system, and set overall objectives for the combined systems. You would allocate a specific amount of trading capital to each system, and develop a risk-management model that takes correlated drawdowns into consideration. In other words, what is the overall risk at any one time you will allow across all your systems?

Let's take a look at how this might work in the following diagram:

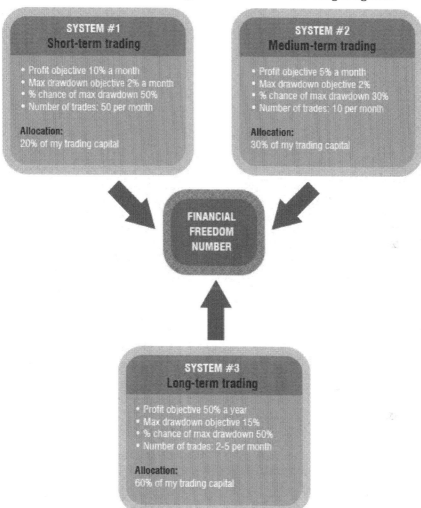

THE BENEFITS OF MULTIPLE SYSTEMS

Having multiple trading systems has several benefits. Firstly, you can satisfy that part of you that wants to go for big wins, by allocating a small part of your capital to a more aggressive approach, while leaving the majority of your money in your other more conservative systems. Secondly, if one system is not working, you could have another that is compensating for it, which increases your returns and stops you from making mistakes. Thirdly, and ideally, you can have multiple trading systems that work in different market types, which you can use or not, depending on current market conditions.

YOUR TURN...

"Defining your style and objectives makes it much easier to stick to your strategy."

~ Mark Minervini

There is no success without action. Setting objectives is something of an art, as they are personal choices about what you want to achieve.

Start by defining the following six objectives:

- Profit objective
- Maximum drawdown
- Chance of maximum drawdown
- Trading opportunity
- Win rate
- Targeted risk/reward ratio

In the next chapter, we will take a deeper look at how you can use position sizing to achieve your objectives.

You Achieve Your Goal Through Position Sizing, Not Your Entry

"So where was he going wrong? Position size. For every one contract I traded he traded ten. He would double his money on two different occasions every year, but still end up flat."

~ Bruce Kovner

"Position sizing is the key to meeting your trading objectives."

~ Van Tharp

"Limit your size in any position so that fear does not become the prevailing instinct guiding your judgement."

~ Joe Vidich

When you're working on your trading strategy, the lure of the charts is tempting. I know I'm guilty of this deadly sin, and my trading has suffered for it. Now it's time for a remedy—to stave off your addiction. It's time to shift your attention away from your charts and onto what actually generates your returns: position sizing.

What Is Position Sizing?

"Your position sizing strategy helps you to determine how much equity to risk on every trade. Its purpose is to help you meet your objectives."

~ Van Tharp

Position sizing is the "how much" part of the equation when you trade Forex. More precisely, it is how much you will buy or sell in each individual position when you place a trade. Or for an expanded definition:

A series of rules about "how much" of each currency you should trade to meet your long-term goals and effectively manage your risk, depending on the quality of your trading system.

A bit of a mouthful, yes. But it's super important. If you can master this idea, it will transform your trading for life. Why? Because it is the number one thing that traders get wrong. It has the power to make or break your trading account.

Trading is an uncertain endeavor. No matter the research you put in or what an expert "says", there is a chance the currency you trade will go against you. Position sizing helps you to preserve your money to fight another day. But it does much more than that. As well as protecting you from risks, position sizing can be used for your own great benefit.

It allows you to:

- Trade more in ideas that have a better potential for reward, or trade more in strong trends.

- To scale into trends in order to build large positions, while keeping your overall risk small.

- To go for big wins while conserving your trading capital, by risking the market's money.

You achieve this by overlaying a position-sizing model or "algorithm" on top of your entry and exit rules.

YOUR POSITION-SIZING MODEL IS AN OVERLAY

"Your trading system employs a set of rules to tell you when and how you trade. The purpose of a trading system is to make sure you can achieve your objectives easily through effective position sizing."

~ Van Tharp

This is one of the most important things to understand about trading Forex: Your position sizing is a completely separate decision from your entry and exit decision. Let's take a look at an example. Say you find a trade you might like to take, risking 50 pips. If the trade goes well, you manage to sell it for 150 pips or three times your potential losses. If the trade goes against you and hits your stop-loss, then you would lose 50 pips: your risk. Pretty simple, right?

Now let's see how applying different position-sizing models to the same trade generates completely different results.

In each model, let's assume you have $10,000 in your Forex trading account.

- Model 1—Number of Lots

  In this model, you decide to buy 1 lot (100K of currency).

  If the trade goes for you, then you would have made 150 x $10, or $1,500. If it goes against you, then you would lose 50 x $10, or $500.

- Model 2—Account Leverage

  In this model, you decide that because you have 100:1 leverage, you will use all of that to take a trade of 10 lots, worth $1,000,000.

  If the trade goes for you, then you would make 150 x $100, or $15,000. If it goes against you, then you would lose 50 x $100, or $5000.

- Model 3—Fixed Percent of Equity Risk

  In this model, you decide to risk 2% of your capital on the trade, or $200.

  This means you buy $40,000 of the currency you are trading.

  If the trade goes for you then you would make 150 x $4 or $600. If it goes against you then you would lose 50 x $4 or $200.

As you can see, the profits or losses on the same trade are altered dramatically, depending on which model you used. This is only the barest bones of the different position-sizing models you could choose to use when you trade Forex. So to reiterate, you can have exactly the same entry and exit and have a completely different result, depending on your position-sizing model. That is why position sizing is so critical. Are you ready to switch your focus to position sizing yet?

HOW TOP TRADERS USE POSITION SIZING TO ACHIEVE THEIR OBJECTIVES

As discussed earlier, top traders think in terms of risk multiples or, as Van Tharp calls them, R-multiples.

Tharp is perhaps the world's number one authority on the concept of position sizing, and is still the ultimate fount of knowledge on the topic. To deep dive into position sizing, the best resource is his *Definitive Guide to Position Sizing*.

R-MULTIPLES ARE CENTRAL TO YOUR POSITION SIZING

When you take a position, your initial risk is the distance between your entry and your stop-loss. This is called your 1R (one times your risk). Through position sizing, you make 1R worth a dollar value or percentage of your account, which finally translates into a number of lots, or micro lots, to buy.

Confused?

Don't worry, we will go into some examples, and with a little bit of practice, R-multiples will soon become second nature.

- Example 1

  You have an account balance of $10,000, and you want to buy the EUR/USD with a 100 pip stop-loss. Your position-sizing model calls for you to risk 2% of your account on the trade, or $200. Your 1R is $200, meaning you should trade 2 mini-lots, or $20,000 (depending on the currency pair you are trading. To work this out, you can use a Forex position-size calculator, which you can find with a quick Google search).

- Example 2

  You have an account balance of $53,000, and you want to short the AUD/USD at 0.8700 with a stop-loss at 0.8750. Your position-sizing model calls for you to risk 1.5% of your account on the trade, or $795. Your 1R is $795, meaning you should trade 10.65 mini lots, or $106,500. Once you have defined your 1R, then your profits are expressed as multiples of this initial risk (R-multiples). For example, if your 1R risk is $795, and you make twice that—$1590—then you would have made 2R. If you made five times your risk—$3975—then you would have made 5R.

HOW POSITION SIZING IS USED TO MEET YOUR OBJECTIVES AND GOALS

Before we get into some specific position-sizing models, I would like to review how some of the decisions you have been making over the past few chapters all come together in the topic of position sizing. As you can see in the following diagram, your broad financial goals, as expressed by your financial freedom number, lead you to develop your trading objectives. To achieve those objectives, you devise a position-sizing model. This, in turn, with the help of R-multiples, tells you exactly how much to trade.

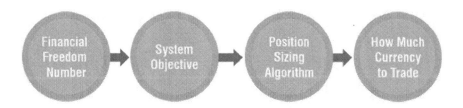

If any of these parts are missing or unclear, then traders tend to struggle with their trading system and either not make as much as they could or lose more than they should.

Each of the system objectives you identified in the previous chapter should be considered when developing your position-sizing model:

- Profit objective

- Maximum drawdown

- Chance of maximum drawdown

- Trading opportunity

- Win rate

- Targeted risk/reward ratio

If, for example, you want to limit your chances of the maximum drawdown, you may trade smaller sizes as you enter into a drawdown. Or, if you have a low win rate, then your position size will need to cater to the inevitable string of losses you will encounter while you wait for the big winning trades to arrive.

YOUR POSITION-SIZING MODEL DEPENDS ON THE QUALITY OF YOUR SYSTEM

The better your system, the larger you can trade, the easier it will be for you to achieve your goals. While you achieve your goals through position sizing, the better your overall trading system is—particularly your entries and exits—the easier it will be for you.

You will be able to:

- Trade larger sizes

- Achieve more consistent returns

- Suffer less drawdowns

- Protect your trading capital

Additionally, it's important to understand that your position-sizing model, while it is independent from your entries and exits, should be logical and relevant to the type and quality of your entries and exits.

HOW TO BUILD A POSITION-SIZING MODEL, A BASIC EXAMPLE

To help this all become clearer, let's work through an example. Say I have a financial freedom number (FFN) of $5000 per month. That is, when I am making $5000 per month on average from my Forex trading, I am financially free.

The objectives I have for my trading system are:

- Profit objective of 10% a month

- No more than a 2% drawdown a month

- A 50% chance of experiencing my maximum drawdown

- 40 trades a month

- 50% win rate with a 3:1 risk/reward ratio.

My trading system has a targeted profit objective of 10%, meaning I would need $50,000 in my Forex trading account to be financially free (50,000 x 10% = $5000 a month profit).

If I can achieve my 50% win rate with a 3:1 risk reward ratio, my trading system has an expectancy of 1 (see chapter 5 to review the concept of expectancy). This means that each time I place a trade, I can expect to make, on average, 1R. Over the course of my 40 trades for the month, I would end up with 40R (40 x 1R).

It can be helpful to think about R as a percentage. For example, if I make 1R, it's 0.5%, 1%, 2% or 3% per R, etc. If I take my 10% profit objective and divide it by 40R, then I get 0.25%. This 0.25% risk is now my position size when I place a trade.

0.25% of my starting capital ($50,000) is $125, meaning each time I trade I would risk $125.

I have a maximum drawdown level of 2%, which I hope to avoid, so I may need to trade smaller at the start of the month until I have some profits. Then I can trade a bigger size; otherwise, it could be too easy to hit my drawdown limit. Note that these choices are discretionary, based on my objectives.

By understanding your broad goal as expressed by your financial freedom number and by extrapolating this into your system objectives, you are able to be very accurate about how much to trade in order to meet your objectives when you enter into a position.

In the real world, you will be faced with a number of subtleties and complexities as you react to the market and the growth or depletion of your account balance. When you are making decisions under these circumstances, always think back to your goals and objectives, and you will find guidance.

A GAME OF MARBLES

"I am wrong all the time. If I can be right 60% of the time, and when I am right, I have some big winners, and when I am wrong, I staunch the losses quickly, I can make a lot of money."

~ Martin Taylor

When I attended a trading course with the aforementioned Van Tharp, we played his "marble game". In this game, trades were simulated by randomly drawing marbles from a bag. While there are several different variations of the game, the basic premise remains the same:

- Each marble pulled from the bag was a trade in R-multiples. In other words, you may lose 1R or make 5R on a pull;

- Everyone had the same amount of starting capital, and they had to risk a certain amount on each pull from the bag;

- There was real money on the table for each game (up to $1200 at one point).

Each pull from the marble bag was considered a trade, and everyone got exactly the same trades. Each simulation lasted at least 30 pulls from the marble bag (trades). There were up to 27 different participants in each game. Okay, just to confirm; everyone had *exactly the same trades*. The systems also tended to have a majority of losing trades, with some big winning trades on occasion. The only control that each participant had was his or her position-sizing rules.

At the end of every game, every single person had different equity, no exceptions. The variation between individuals was massive, from bankrupt through to several million dollars' profit. After playing the game a few times, it became very apparent how position sizing is not only composed of an entry and exit, with a separate position-sizing model applied on top. It was also very apparent that here are a huge variety of potential position-sizing models you can choose from to meet your objectives.

Let's take a look at some now.

If you are interested in playing the marble game for yourself, Van Tharp lets you play for free on his website. I highly recommended this game to help you gain an in-depth understanding of position sizing.

MODEL 1—PERCENT OF EQUITY RISK PER TRADE

With this position-sizing model, you risk a fixed percentage of your account balance on each trade. For example, you might risk 1 or 2% on each trade. That is, if the trade goes against you, then you lose 1 or 2% of your account. There are a number of variations you can take when using this model. For instance:

- Percent of starting balance—you risk a fixed percentage of your starting balance.

- Percent of current equity—you risk a fixed percentage of your current account balance at the time you place the trade.

- Percent of equity high—you risk a fixed percentage of the highest point of your account balance.

While the differences here may seem subtle, they can lead to quite different performance over time.

MODEL 2—MARKET'S MONEY

"The way to build long-term returns is through preservation of capital and home runs. You can be far more aggressive when you're making good profits"

~ Stanley Druckenmiller

"When I am more attuned to the market and playing with market money, I will increase my position size."

~ Scott Ramsey

I'm sure you have heard how important it is to protect your initial trading capital. You will have also heard about how some people become very rich trading currencies with very little money. This is where a market's money position-sizing model can help. With a market's money position-sizing model, you use profits you have made to trade larger positions, while trading small with your own core trading capital. For example, say you have a $100,000 account, you risk 0.25-0.5% of your account per trade, but when your account gets into a profit, you risk 2-5% or more to trade larger sizes. This way, you limit the risks on your initial capital, yet you can still go for big wins when the opportunity presents itself.

One question you will need to answer is this: when does the market's money become your money? That is, when do you lock in your profits and consider them part of your core capital? You could do this based on:

- A time period, such as a year
- A profit objective, such as 50%
- A combination of the two

Have a think about how you would feel risking some of your profits to make large gains, and see if it would suit you. It's important that you don't start to engage in risky trading behavior when you are using the market's money, just because it's not "yours." Market's money is to be used in a controlled fashion.

MODEL 3—SCALE IN TO THE TREND

"The Trend is Your Friend."

~ Trading Adage

A scale-in position-sizing model takes advantage of trends to add to winning positions.

As your trade goes into profit, you add additional smaller positions to create one large position. As you add positions, you would move your stop-loss to keep your risk on the overall position small (1R or less). This way, if a trade goes for you, then you could have a big win, but at no time are you exposed to a large loss.

For example, when you see your initial entry, you buy your first position, risking 1% of your account. Once the currency pair goes up in price, you add another position, and move the original stop-loss up. You then continue to add positions and trail the stop-loss up until you have your core position. As the trade continues to go up, you trail the stop-loss higher until you eventually have a large position that is essentially "risk free", or with locked-in profit, because your stop-loss is above your entry points.

Remember, you don't want to be scaling into losing positions. Paul Tudor Jones, a market wizard, has a plaque on his wall that reads, "loser's average losers", so don't be that guy or girl. Note that this is different from splitting your position into two or three parts, and legging into a trade as it goes against you, while keeping a fixed stop-loss on the position. In the first scenario of adding to a loser, your losses keep growing bigger and bigger as the trade moves against you. In the second case, where you split your position, your losses actually end up smaller as you effectively have less risk than if you went in 100% at market.

DIFFERENT TYPES OF TRADES

"Varying position sizes can be as important as the entry methodology. Trading smaller, or not at all for lower probability trades, and larger for higher probability trades can transform a losing strategy into a winning one."

~ Jack Schwager, discussing insights from Edward Thorp

Good traders adjust their position sizing based on the timeframe of the trade. If they are more active, they tend to risk a smaller amount per trade; whereas, traders who take a longer-term approach will be comfortable with a larger degree of risk on the position. You can consider trading with different levels of risk, depending on the timeframe of the trade. For example, you may risk more on a longer-term trade and less on a shorter-term trade.

CONFIDENCE AND CONVICTION LEVELS

It makes sense to trade smaller when you are not in form or in touch with the markets, and to trade bigger when a great trade is lining up, or you are on a hot streak. This is a critical difference between the amateur trader and the professional. The professional knows when he or she is on form, and it is a good time to swing big. The amateurs treat all trades the same. This results in the amateur trader never winning as big as they could if they sized their positions in line with their conviction levels.

MILESTONE AND GOALS

When you achieve certain goals or milestones, you may want to adjust your position sizing. For example, if you hit your monthly goal, what will you do? Will you stop trading? Reduce your position size? Perhaps you will decide to swing big, using some of your monthly profit-to-date as market's money.

Milestones are important points to note on the way to your goals. For example, if you get close to your goal for the month, you might decide to trade smaller to avoid turning a winning month into a losing one.

Nothing Influences Your Success More Than Position Sizing

"90% of performance variation among professional traders is due to position sizing strategies."

~ Van Tharp

Take your thoughts on position sizing, and put them down on paper. How well you answer the questions will have a significant impact on your success, so take your time, and do it thoroughly. As always, remember you can change your model in the future as you learn more, so if you are feeling stuck in an area, simply move on.

Four Different Approaches to Forex Trading

While there are dozens—or maybe even hundreds—of specific approaches to trading, the majority of Forex traders fit into one of four main categories. Let's look at them now.

Impulse Trading

Impulse trading means trading based on some form of very basic analysis but with no real objectives in mind. An impulse trader could probably give you a basic justification for any of their trades, but more likely, they couldn't tell you what they really hoped to achieve.

'Am I an impulse trader?'

Ever see a candlestick pattern you like—such as a hammer—and get so excited about it that you just *have* to place a trade? (Only to be disappointed when it goes against you?)

If this is you, then you are likely an impulse trader. Impulse trading does not mean trading with no structure; rather, it is trading with some form of basic analysis and no, or very limited, objectives.

Impulse traders may even have detailed trading plans, but when they are trading, they enter as soon as they see something half-decent. Another sign that you are an impulse trader might be if you hit your monthly loss limit in the first few days of the month, or if you have a lot of correlated trades on at the same time that go against you. Your impulses and lack of clarity have caused you to overtrade.

MECHANICAL TRADERS OR EXPERT ADVISORS (EAS)

Mechanical trading is when you program a piece of software to trade on your behalf. In the Forex space, these *robots* are often referred to as Expert Advisors (EAs), after one of the more popular pieces of trading software in the industry—Metatrader 4. In reality, there are a variety of different software packages that cater to an automated trading approach.

Mechanical trading has its benefits. It eliminates some of the psychological issues traders may have—such as an inability to pull the trigger on entries. It also allows traders to manage their time more efficiently, as they don't have to watch the trading screen very intently. Often, there is no requirement at all to oversee your robot directly.

Mechanical trading does have its downsides. The robot is unable to adapt to changes in market conditions so may stop working properly if the market changes drastically. Additionally, since it relies on computer code to function, any software issues will cause complications.

With a good trading plan, sensible risk management, and properly implemented failsafe procedures, there is still an excellent case to be made for using Expert Advisors to trade. It demands research and good judgment, but it works.

Typically, mechanical traders are engaged in a research war. You need to keep evolving your mechanical system, so it continues to work in the current market environment. It is very easy to "curve-fit" a mechanical system so that it worked well in the past, but it's much more difficult to produce one that works well in real-time.

RULES-BASED DISCRETIONARY TRADING

Van Tharp suggests that 90% of successful traders are rules-based, discretionary traders, with the remaining 10% being mechanical traders.

A *rules-based discretionary trader* has a set of rules, based on their market model, for implementing winning trades. The system at the end of this book is a rules-based discretionary system. An example of a rules-based discretionary system might be:

"When the price is trading below the 10-period daily EMA, go to a 1-hour chart, and enter on break below the lower Bollinger Band, after a period of consolidation at least 12 bars long."

The challenge that I have with a rules-based system is that it's considered a mistake to stray from your rules, and so you can feel bound to apply them even when you can see it makes little sense to do so.

In some cases, your rules simply won't fit the current context or sentiment. Sometimes, the market is quite clearly turning (or has quite clearly turned) against you, and yet your *rules* would still have you place a trade anyway.

Another challenge with a rules-based approach is that many traders feel they need to "back-test" their ideas. Back-testing is generally done by placing indicators on historical chart data to see how well your indicators (and thus your *idea*) would have worked in the past.

While this may seem logical and valid, it can get confusing. A simplified set of rules that can be back-tested does not really encompass the variety of market types and conditions we intuitively observe as traders.

This leaves the trader feeling incomplete, so they tinker with their rules constantly. Worse, this tinkering is often based on "recency bias"—making changes based on the last thing that happened to us—and sometimes ends up over-complicating the rules altogether. This is almost guaranteed to backfire and cause confusion in the heat of battle, as simplicity and clarity are what's called for when trading in the moment.

For this reason, I prefer an evolution of the rules-based approach. It's called *process-driven, objective-based* trading, and it allows you to encompass a much greater variety of inputs seamlessly, while trading what is going on in front of you.

PROCESS-DRIVEN, OBJECTIVE-BASED TRADING

The approach I use for my trading (mostly) and that we use for our signals with my business, FX Renew, is process-driven and objective-based. You can see the performance we have generated for our signals using this approach. At the time of writing, we have a 38% return with no greater than a 4% draw-down. This is not using any sort of martingale approach. It is simply a year and a half of good trading decisions.

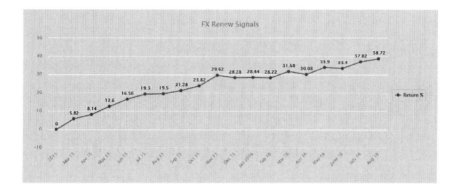

Rather than follow a strict set of rules, in a process-driven approach, you follow a disciplined routine for analyzing the market and then develop conviction in what you want to trade. Then—and this is a simple idea—you pick your best idea to trade.

To give an example, each Sunday, I sit down and spend 3-4 hours going through a series of reports and charts to determine what I think the opportunities are for the coming week. You can get this report for free on the FX Renew Blog.

Here are the things I consider:

- Risk sentiment. I look at the stock market to determine whether we are in a risk-on or risk-off environment.

- Commodity correlations. For example, gold and copper are important to the AUD. Milk powder is important to the NZD and Oil to the CAD.

- Bond correlations. There is a close relationship between bonds and currencies.

- Strength vs. other currencies. If you are looking to buy a currency, does it show strength across the board, or is the signal a noisy blip on just one pair?

- Risk vs. reward. Does the opportunity fit my risk/reward parameters?

- Trade timeframe. Is the opportunity short term or long term? Do I expect a big move?

- Market type. The trade should be the appropriate one for the current market type, and the market type you expect to follow next.

- Big-picture global macro. Does the trade line up with the global macro environment? (This may not be so relevant for short-term trades.)

- Technical quality (set-up). How good is the technical set-up? Are there any candlestick or technical patterns that indicate future direction? What do my indicators tell me?

- Short-term news flow/fundamental catalyst. Is there a news event that has triggered the trade?

- Sentiment. What big thing is the market focusing on right now? For example, is it yield, is it risk-off, or is it a macro event such as Brexit?

- Upcoming news. Are there any news events on the horizon that could impact the trade? What do you expect the outcome of the event to be?

- Gut feeling (do you like it?). Do you have a good feeling about the trade? Does it seem like the right trade to take, or are you forcing it?

Once I have written down my conclusions, I then take a break and think about what I want to trade, given my objectives for the coming week and my risk management framework. The break is important as it allows for greater objectivity and clarity.

Once I have decided what to trade, I draw on my knowledge (outlined in this book), and plan the best approach for implementing the trades I have chosen. For example, where should my entries be? Should I be all in at market price or scale-in to my position? How should I exit?

Then I scenario plan. For example, if I am long NZD/USD, what do I do if stocks break out to the downside, or the dairy auction has a bad miss? What do I do with my position in relation to the upcoming news this week?

Once I have taken the trade, I keep my objectives for the position in mind. I also trade what is in front of me by staying vigilant for changes in the market type, price action, and sentiment, etc.

The next Sunday, I repeat, and do exactly the same thing. Then each day, the traders and I run our own processes for selecting our day trades for the signals. The key, I have found, is the hard work that happens before you trade because it allows you to make effective decisions when you have large sums of money on the line.

This means you can operate in the market using the full spectrum of knowledge you have, within a disciplined, risk-management framework, in order to achieve your trading goals. This style of trading allows you to avoid being constrained by rules that are not necessarily relevant to what is going on in front of you.

The Key to Forex System Development Market Types

"It's insane to expect that same system to work well in all market types."

~ Van Tharp

Perhaps the biggest mistake traders make when they build their Forex trading system has to do with market types. Traders tend to put blinkers on, and use the same approach, no matter what the market is doing in front of them. But it is very difficult to have a winning trading system that works well in all conditions. Your system might work well in trending markets and perform poorly in sideways markets—so why trade it in sideways markets? The simple solution is to identify the market type first, and then apply a strategy that works in that market type.

Primary Market Types

"Successful traders adapt to changing market conditions."

~ Jack Schwager, discussing insights from Edward Thorp

Van Tharp, a Market Wizard and expert on the subject, suggests that there are as many as 26 market types. You will see this, too, as you get more experienced in identifying them. Sometimes, it's difficult to work out an exact classification for the market type, but don't let that set you back—close enough is good enough. In my Forex trading, I tend to use six primary market types:

- Bull normal
- Bull volatile
- Bear normal
- Bear volatile
- Sideways quiet
- Sideways volatile

There are several methods of identifying market types. Van Tharp uses a mechanical market-type classification system that applies an algorithm to market direction and volatility. I prefer to use charts when trading Forex (more on this below). You can see the primary market types here on the weekly chart of the JPY/USD:

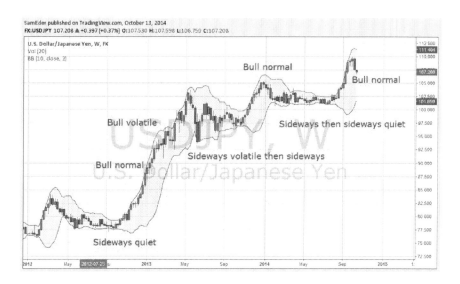

Now it's your turn. How many market types can you spot on this chart?

Here is what I can find:

Can you see how it would be difficult to trade the same way in all these market types?

SHIFTING MARKET TYPES TRADING TRANSITIONS

Like the sea turns from calm to stormy, so do the markets. One of the tricks to using market types is knowing what to expect next. Trading is very much about probabilities, and if you know which market type(s) will likely follow next, then it can give you a big edge. Here are the primary market types and an indication of what often comes next:

- Bull normal. Followed by a bull volatile or sideways quiet.

- Bull volatile. Followed by a sideways volatile or a bear volatile

- Bear normal. Followed by a bear volatile or a sideways quiet

- Bear volatile. Followed by a bull volatile or a sideways volatile

- Sideways quiet. Followed by a bull or bear normal or a sideways volatile

93

- Sideways volatile. Followed by a bull or bear normal or a sideways quiet.

So if you are in a bull normal market, you can expect a bull volatile to happen next, and then you can be wary in a bull volatile that it could quickly drop into a bear volatile, and you can plan appropriately.

POSITION SIZING IN DIFFERENT MARKET TYPES

"Traders...need to adjust position size in response to the changing market environment."

~ *Jack Schwager, discussing insights from Steve Clark*

Market types play an important part in your position sizing. You may not necessarily need to stop trading a strategy in a market type in which it does not work so well. Rather, you can simply reduce the position size. Similarly, if you have a strategy that works very well in a certain market type, you could then trade much bigger sizes when in that market type.

AN EASY-TO-USE TECHNIQUE FOR IDENTIFYING MARKET TYPES

To identify market types in Forex, I use the Bollinger Bands. You can use this technique on weekly charts, daily charts, hourly charts, or whatever timeframe suits you. I tend to use the daily chart to identify the market type, though I often stalk entries off the hourly or 4-hour charts. The shorter your trading horizon, the lower the timeframe you will use to identify market types.

I use the standard 20-period, 2-deviation Bollinger bands. When the Bollinger Bands are expanded slightly, it is a sign of a normally trending market type. When they are stretched, it is a sign of a volatile market type. When they are contracted, it is a sign of a quiet market type.

If the price is trending in the direction of the upper or lower Bollinger Bands, then that will indicate a bull or bear market. If the price is between the two bands without clear direction, the market type is sideways.

If you combine these two factors, you can normally identify the market type pretty easily.

While Bollinger Bands are very useful, market type identification can be improved by using price action.

PICKING THE MARKET TYPE WITH PRICE ACTION

Price action will allow you to identify bull volatile or bear volatile market types better than the Bollinger Bands, and it can also help you to get in on market type transitions early. Bull volatile and bear volatile markets can be identified simply by increasingly long candles or bars.

The switch from a bullish to bearish market type—and vice versa—can be quite rapid. Price action can be used to identify this switch, as the market type will often change direction when it hits a significant support and resistance level. You can look for candlestick reversals off weekly support and resistance levels, or double tops and bottoms, for a sign of the change in market type direction.

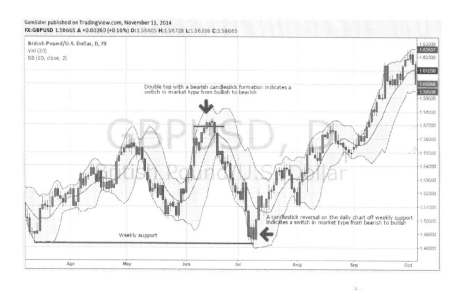

Just be very aware of what is going on, as reversals don't always work out, and the original direction could resume with a vengeance!

STRATEGIES FOR DIFFERENT MARKET TYPES

"When you have a trading system, you should always know how it performs under various market conditions."

~ Van Tharp

Van Tharp believes that it's nigh on impossible to build a Holy Grail system that works in all market types, but it's not that difficult to build one that works well in a particular market type. His suggestion is that traders develop a number of non-correlated systems that work well in different market types. This is generally a good idea, as it will help improve your consistency. As a discretionary trader, I will always be analyzing the current market type and conditions and thinking about what the best approach to employ is based on the outline below.

Let's take a brief look at each market type and a strategy that you can apply in each one.

- Bull Normal

    To identify a bull normal market type, look for the price to be trending with the upper band and above the mid Bollinger Band. Generally, bull normal market types suit trend-following strategies. Look for a pullback or a consolidation phase, followed by the breakout in the direction of the trend.

- Bull Volatile

    In a bull volatile market type, you will see long, bullish bars or candles when the price trends with the upper band. The price may frequently cross above the upper band. Bull volatile market types can suit short-term swing-trading strategies. Stops should be kept tight and profits left to run for some strong risk/reward trades. Additionally, bull volatile market types often occur prior to market tops.

- Bear Normal

  Bear normal is the opposite of bull normal. The price trends with the lower bands and remains below the mid band. Like the bull normal market type, look for pullbacks to key levels and consolidation phases followed by a breakout in the direction of the trend.

- Bear Volatile

  Bear volatile is the opposite of bull volatile. You will see long, bearish bars develop that sometimes cross below the lower band. As in the bull volatile, look for swing-trading opportunities in the direction of the trend with tight stops, and let profits run. Additionally, bear volatile market types often occur prior to market tops.

- Sideways Volatile

  In a sideways volatile market type, the bands are wide, and there is large, sideways price movement. Sideways volatile markets suit a band-trading approach. Look for prices to get to the edge of the band, and fade the move back toward the opposite edge of the band.

- Sideways Quiet

  In a sideways quiet market type, the bands contract, and the price forms a tight range. Many traders find sideways quiet market types difficult, but they can be very lucrative if you are patient enough to wait for the breakout. Alternatively, you could go down to a lower timeframe, and apply a band-trading approach.

ADVANCED MARKET TYPES

I have also developed some advanced market type classifications. You can read about them on the FX Renew blog.

TRADE IN THE MOMENT WITH MARKET TYPES

"It's easy to design a good system that works well in any one market type."

~ *Van Tharp*

Building a winning Forex trading system does not have to be difficult, but it will be if you don't use market types. Instead of focusing your time on trying to find a unicorn—the trading strategy that works in every market type—build a system for identifying the market type, and apply a simple, low-risk/high-reward trading strategy that fits. Take some time now to add the Bollinger Bands to your favorite currency pairs, and identify the market type you are in right now.

Damn Good Forex Set-Ups

"Luck is what happens when preparation meets opportunity."

~ Seneca (Roman philosopher)

"I like to go for cinches. I like to shoot fish in a barrel. But I like to do it after the water has run out."

~ Warren Buffett

Set-ups stack the probabilities in your favor. The better your set-up, the greater the chance of having a winning trade. The more winning trades you have, the easier it will be to achieve your objectives through your position-sizing model. In this chapter, we go through several set-ups you can add to your trading plan.

Set-ups Are Not Entries

It's important to note that a set-up is not an entry. Once you see your set-up, you then go into "stalking mode", and wait for your entry to appear. It's all about optimizing the risk-to-reward profile of the trade. If you are patient, you will generally be able to find an entry level that lets you have a tighter stop-loss. Sometimes, this may mean you miss out on getting into a position, as the entry does not materialize, but you are not looking to take every trade—only the ones that really stack up.

Of course, you can place a trade when you see a set-up, and some set-ups require you to, but often, you will be better waiting for the opportune moment to enter.

A RISK/REWARD FILTER FOR YOUR TRADES

When you assess a set-up, you want to determine if the risk/reward is right for you. To do this, you can use a risk/reward filter. The concept behind a risk/reward filter is that you don't place a trade unless the potential reward is greater than the risk by a certain amount. For example, you might not take a trade unless the potential is to make at least three times profit compared to the risk.

Generally, it's best practice to look for a risk/reward of at least 1:3 on long-term trades. Paul Tudor Jones suggests going for 5:1, and Bill Lipschutz suggests you need to work out how to make money if you are only right 20% of the time. For short-term trades, it's acceptable to have a much lower risk/reward ratio. This could be even less than 1R if the win rate is high, and the losses are kept smaller than 1R, too.

It is important to note here that simply moving your stop-loss tighter or your profit target farther away in order to "manufacture" a risk/reward ratio of 3:1 will not work. What you are looking for are genuine opportunities for trades that have a superior risk/reward. Don't make this mistake, or you will find your targets don't get hit, but your stop-losses do.

A WORD OF CAUTION

"What really matters is the long-run distribution of outcomes from your trading techniques, systems, and procedures. But, psychologically, what seems of paramount importance is whether the positions that you have right now are going to work. Current positions that you have, beyond any statistical justification. It's quite tempting to bend your rules to make your current trades work, assuming that the favorability of your long-term statistics will take care of future profitability. Two of the cardinal sins of trading—giving too much rope and taking profits prematurely—are both attempts to make current positions more likely to succeed, to the severe detriment of long-term performance."

~ William Eckhardt

Set-ups can be very entrancing. It's easy to get sucked down the rabbit hole and spend far too much time on this aspect of your trading plan. As a general rule, you want to spend 10-15% of your system-development process time on set-ups and entries.

You also want to be very clear on your objectives. If you are looking for long-term trades, then your set-up should be congruent and vice versa with short-term trades. Too many traders make the mistake of using set-ups that don't suit their objectives, and this results in them cutting their losses short or getting stopped out far too often. For example, if you are looking for long-term moves of several hundred pips, your set-up should be developed on a higher timeframe, such as weekly or daily. It's no good looking for a set-up on an hourly chart if you're trading for the long term—though you can go down to the hourly chart to stalk an entry. (More on this later).

Combined Set-ups

"Fundamentalists who say they are not going to pay any attention to the charts are like a doctor who says he's not going to take a patient's temperature."

~ Bruce Kovner

While you can trade effectively using a set-up on its own, often, your probability of success on the trade will improve if you can combine one or more high-probability set-ups with another. For example, if you have sentiment in your favor and then you get an excellent technical set-up that supports your view, your trade could be much better than if you are only trading off a technical pattern.

Some Damn Good Set-ups

"Sometimes the opportunities are so obvious that you almost can't lose when they come around; the only problem is that they don't come around that often. The key is not to lose money in the times in between."

~ Stuart Walton

If you pick up any book on Forex trading, it is likely packed full to the brim with set-ups. In general, you will find a lot of them work, and they will give you an edge. What the books probably don't cover are the position-sizing and trade-management techniques you need to turn that edge into profits. Nor will they advise you that the set-up only work in some market conditions and not others.

It would be impractical for me to cover anywhere near the number of set-ups you will come across throughout your trading career, and if you learn or have learned ones from elsewhere that fit you, then that is fine, as well.

Set-ups generally fall within two categories:

- Technical
- Fundamental

Let's look at few of these now.

TECHNICAL ANALYSIS SET-UPS

"I haven't met a rich technician."

~ Jim Rogers

"I always laugh at people who say 'I've never met a rich technician' I love that it's such an arrogant, nonsensical response. I used fundamentals for 9 years and got rich as a technician."

~ Marty Schwartz

Technical set-ups are based on chart analysis. Charts are windows into the soul of your trade, and fortunes have been made by their application.

But charts can also be very easily misunderstood by the newbie, who tends to make things much more complex than they need to be. The trick with chart analysis is to keep things simple, look for low risk/high reward entries in alignment with the bigger picture of market type, fundamentals, and sentiment, and then focus on managing the trade after you get into it (a topic of an upcoming chapter).

TECHNICAL INDICATORS

"The 10 day exponential moving average (EMA) is my favourite indicator to determine the major trend. I call this "red light, green light" because it is imperative in trading to remain on the correct side of a moving average to give yourself the best probability of success. When you are trading above the 10 day, you have the green light, the market is in positive mode and you should be thinking buy. Conversely, trading below the average is a red light. The market is in a negative mode and you should be thinking sell."

~ Marty Schwartz

One of the most common ways to use charts is to use technical indicators such as Moving Averages, Bollinger Bands or Stochastic Oscillators. While these indicators are too numerous to go into in this lesson, let's look at some best practice around how you use an indicator in system development. The indicator needs to have a purpose. You should not add an indicator to a chart unless it helps you do something specific. For example, you might apply the ADX to confirm a trend, or use a Parabolic SAR as a trailing stop.

The indicator should not cause confusion. Many traders apply too many indicators to their charts, and the indicators conflict with each other. While it can be good to have two indicators confirm a set-up, adding three can just cause confusion and indecision, which is the last thing you want when you are trading.

Keep in mind that Indicators are *fictional*. Ultimately, indicators are just lines on a chart. They are not real. Just because your indicator gives you a buy signal does not mean that anything has actually happened. The markets are driven by supply and demand and will move based on market orders, not your indicator. While indicators can be immensely useful, it is worth keeping the idea that indicators are fictional very much in mind and to remember to practice risk management.

It pays to get to know your indicator. Rather than chopping and changing indicators, it can be good to get to know your indicator intimately. Learn to use it on different settings, timeframes, and currency pairs.

Example: The MACD Indicator on a GBPJPY chart.

Support and Resistance (Key Levels)

Support and resistance levels indicate previous price levels where buyers or sellers have stepped into the market, and price has changed direction. If a level has held in the past, it can be an indication a level will hold again in the future. Support and resistance can make good set-ups, as the price often reverses off these levels.

The higher the timeframe, the more powerful the support and resistance level. Support and resistance that shows up on weekly charts can signal important turning points.

Daily and Weekly Pivot Points

The concept behind pivot points is that, more often than not, price will stay inside the "reversal zone". In a sideways market type, the price moves from one pivot point to another. There's a whole scholarly discussion on pivot points and how price action moves between them. Pivot points can be used as set-ups in both trending and sideways market types.

CHART PATTERNS

Chartists use classic, technical analysis patterns to time the markets. These patterns help a trader recognize the supply and demand factors that drive the markets and are often reflections of market psychology. The patterns listed below are some of the more common ones:

- Symmetrical Triangles.

- Ascending Triangles.

- Descending Broadening Wedge.

- Ascending Wedge.

- Head and Shoulders.

- Inverse Head and Shoulders.

There is plenty of literature for you to dive deep into chart patterns if you want to learn more, so I won't go into detail here. Suffice to say, chart patterns still hold true in this day and age.

BIG MONEY CAN BE MADE BY THE CONTRARIAN PICKING TOPS AND BOTTOMS

"I consider myself a premier market opportunist. That means I develop an idea on the market and pursue it from a very low-risk stand-point until I have repeatedly been proven wrong, or until I change my viewpoint."

~ Paul Tudor Jones

Picking tops and bottoms is not for the faint-hearted. You need to be prepared to take the opposite view to the crowd, and fearlessly buy when others are selling. You also need to be flexible enough to admit when you are incorrect. The trading landscape is littered with ego-driven traders who refused to believe they were wrong. The market cares little for your views...

But if you do manage to get in on a top or bottom, then you can stand to make very large returns. To pick the turning points, you can look for double tops and bottoms or head and should patterns. If you see one of these, it could be a sign the market is set to change direction, and this makes quite a good set-up. If you are looking to pick tops and bottoms, don't expect to get it right the first time. It might take you several goes before the direction goes for you, so keep your risk management tight.

CONSOLIDATIONS

The Forex market expands and contracts from periods of volatility to quiet periods. These periods of quiet can make excellent set-ups, as when the market expands, the moves can be rapid and the risk vs. reward excellent. These periods of consolidation happen across numerous timeframes, from weekly, right down to several times per day.

CORRELATIONS WITH BONDS

Bond prices have a major impact on currency pairs. Remember, when you are trading currencies, you are essentially trading cash deposits. These deposits earn you interest if you are long, and you need to pay interest if you are short.

Bond prices move based on interest rates, so if interest rates go up, then bond prices drop and vice versa. So, for example, if T-bonds drop in value, it is bullish for the USD. If German Bunds drop in value, it is bullish for the EUR. These relationships can be a little complex, but it is worth taking note. Search for "bonds" on the FX Renew blog for more information.

CORRELATIONS WITH STOCK INDICES (RISK ON/RISK OFF)

There are often correlations between what is going on in the stock market and what happens in currencies. Essentially when stocks are going up, it is termed "risk-on", which is bullish for higher yielding currencies, such as AUD, NZD, and TRY.

When stocks are going down, it is termed "risk-off", which is bearish for the above currencies and bullish for JPY and USD. This is also bullish for other carry trade "funding" currencies (currencies with low interest rates).

COMMODITIES

Commodity prices play an important part in the economics of some currencies. For example, the AUD is heavily influenced by the prices of iron ore and gold. The NZD is influenced by the price of dairy products—specifically milk powder. The Canadian dollar is greatly impacted by the price of oil.

OTHER CURRENCIES COMPONENT PARTS

One currency may also influence another, particularly if these economies are closely related. It is common for the EUR and GBP to be correlated, as it is for the AUD and NZD.

Experienced traders look at not only the currency pair they are trading, but also check to see how the currency they are planning to trade is performing against other currencies. Ideally, a trader might trade the strongest vs. the weakest currency pairs.

Finally, they want to make sure they like the component part of each trade. If I am trading a cross, for example, buying GBPAUD, I want to make sure I'd like to buy GBPUSD, and I'd like to sell AUDUSD. If I'd like to sell GBPUSD and buy AUDUSD, then it would not make sense to buy GBPAUD.

TIME OF DAY

Time of day is a very important set-up that traders often neglect. If you can place trades at optimal times that suit your strategy, then it can improve your edge. Due to the twenty-four-hour nature of the Forex markets, money flows in to currency pairs at different times, depending on market opening hours in the US, UK, and Japan. During times of money flow, you might expect to experience more breakouts, while during quiet times you might expect the market to range trade more. This does not always hold true, though; if a trend gets going during quiet, illiquid times, then it can be a wild ride with no volume to hold it back.

Forex Money Flow (GMT Time)

- Tokyo 12:00 a.m. Tokyo money flow

- 6:30 a.m.-7:15 a.m. pre-London

- 8:00 a.m. London open

- 12:20 p.m.-12:40 p.m. pre-New York (early New York money & professional traders)

- 1:00 p.m.-1:30 p.m. New York open (banks, pits, etc.)

- 1:30 p.m. money flow stock market open

- 1:45 p.m.-2:15 a.m. daily spot-trade

- 5:00 p.m. money exit

High probability trades can be found when there is strong support or resistance at market opens.

FUNDAMENTAL SET-UPS

"I develop a macro view about something, but then there are 20 different ways I can play it. The key question is: What gives me the best risk/reward?"

~ Michael Platt

Fundamental set-ups are based on supply and demand factors. Generally, the more a currency is in demand, the more it will strengthen. Sentiment also plays a major role. Sentiment is the fundamental factor the market is focusing on right now (more on sentiment in a tick).

Fundamental analysis of currencies is, like technical analysis, an immense topic. It is also tricky, as the market often "prices in" the fundamentals, so when you get news you think is positive for the currency, it may actually go down. This is to say that certain assumptions are sometimes already in play. For example: if the market expects the New Zealand central bank interest rate to rise by .5%, and it only rises by .25%, the price of NZD may actually fall, even though the interest rate rose. More on this below.

THE CRITICAL IMPORTANCE OF UNDERSTANDING MARKET SENTIMENT

"What is important is to assess what the market is focusing on at the given moment."

~ Bill Lipschutz

This quote sums up *sentiment* in a nutshell—the Forex market is highly psychological, and it is quite often the prevailing *current perception* that drives the market. To a certain extent, if the market *believes* it is happening, then it *is* happening.

Understanding what the market is focusing on will take you a long way. Think about the bearish JPY trend in 2012—the market was focused on the Bank of Japan and Abenomics. The bear trend in the EUR in 2014 was because the markets were focused on the Greek Debt Crisis. In 2016, the GBP sold off for months, as the focus was on BREXIT.

Sentiment is not always big picture, either. You want to understand what the market is focusing on for that day or week. As Lipschutz says, "One day the foreign exchange market may be focusing on interest rate differentials; the next day the market may be looking at the potential for capital appreciation, which is exactly the opposite."

INTEREST RATES AND CENTRAL BANK POLICY

"A counter to anticipated response to market news may be more meaningful than the news item itself. Platt recalls a trade in which there was a continuing stream of adverse news. He repeatedly expected to lose money after each news item, and yet the market did not move against him. Platt read the inability of the market to respond to the news as confirmation of his trade idea, and he quadrupled his position, turning it into one of his biggest winners ever."

~ Jack Schwager, author of Market Wizards, discussing lessons from Michael Platt

You can think of currencies a little like bank deposits and loans. For example, if you buy the AUD, then it is like having a deposit in an account in AUD, from which you earn interest. If you are selling it against the USD, it would be like having a loan in USD, on which you pay interest. If you earn more interest than you pay, then you have a positive carry—in other words, you will earn money just for holding your position. From a trading perspective, it can make sense to own the currencies that are paying you interest, and sell those that don't.

Inflation and deflation can have a significant impact on the long-term performance of currency pairs. If more currency is being created due to inflation, then supply of the currency pair increases. If currency is being destructed due to deflation, then it decreases supply of a currency pair. Keep these factors in mind when looking for long-term moves.

Finally, central banks around the globe have begun programs of quantitative easing (money printing), which impact the supply and demand of currencies. Because of this, the actions of central banks around the globe are heavily scrutinized, and their policies can be significant drivers of movement in currency pairs. But it is not all as simple as it may seem. Even if a central bank is printing money, the currency may strengthen due to debt deflation or money supply.

As a Forex trader, recognize that interest rates and other central bank policies can be very good set-ups for trades. A good example was in the Japanese Yen (JPY) in 2013-14, where the Bank of Japan was aggressively easing monetary policy, leading to some very good trading opportunities.

NEWS EVENTS

"Fundamentals that you read about are typically useless, as the market has already discounted the price. I call them funny-mentals. However, if you catch on early, before others believe, then you might have valuable surprise-a-mentals."

~ Ed Seykota

The trading week will be peppered with data releases and other news events, some more important than others. This could be interest rate announcements, speeches from officials, or economic data releases, such as GDP or employment numbers. One of the main news event traders watch for is Non-From Payrolls (NFP), which is the US employment report. Note that you are not only looking at news in the country of the currency you are trading. For example, China news will impact the Australian and New Zealand dollars, and US news has implications for most currencies given its global significance.

News will often serve to reverse or continue a trend, so it pays to know what upcoming news events are of significance to the currencies you are trading. You can find out what events are due and the expected outcome in bank reports (see the resources page on FX Renew). If the news is different from what the market expects (a surprise), it can lead to swings in the currency price. Note that algorithms run by hedge funds also play a role in the trading around news events, often causing wild, sometimes irrational swings, immediately as news is released.

There are plenty of ways to use news as a set-up. Some traders will:

- Look to predict the news event's outcome, and place a trade beforehand.
- Wait for the news event, and enter the trade based on the announcement (be wary of slippage).
- Wait for the reaction to the news event, and place the trade several minutes or hours after. You may even want to wait for the close of the trading day in New York.

All are valid strategies; you just need to choose the one that appeals to you and gives you an edge.

YOUR TURN

"I think investment psychology is by far the more important element, followed by risk control, with the least important consideration being the question of where you buy and sell."

~ Tom Basso

"[It's] not some magical source that is the key to the markets, as most people believe. The metaphor of the "Holy Grail"... is all about finding yourself."

~ Van Tharp

Select some damn good set-ups for your trading system. You want to make sure they:

- Fit your psychology
- Fit the other elements of your system
- Give you an edge

Make sure you don't just settle for the easy option. Technical analysis can be seductive because it's simple to get started and intriguing to many traders, but you will find that by understanding market sentiment, knowing what news could drive the price, and being clear on the big picture fundamentals, your edge will be much greater.

How to Stalk a Low Risk/High Reward Entry Point

"Although the cheetah is the fastest animal in the world, and can catch any animal on the plains, it will wait until it is absolutely sure it can catch its prey. It may hide in the bush for a week, waiting for just the right moment. It will wait for a baby antelope, and not just any baby antelope, but preferably one that is also sick or lame; only then, when there is no chance it can lose its prey does it attack. That to me is the epitome of professional trading."

~ Mark Weinstein

You've done your homework. You've found a damn good set-up, and now it's time to execute. The temptation is to jump in straight away. But now is the time for patience. It's time to stalk your entry like the cheetah stalks its prey.

As a Forex trader, you should have an array of simple entries at your disposal that help you enter into your chosen positions during low risk and high reward times. This improves the odds of having a winning trade, while at the same time maximizing rewards and minimizing risks, which is the goal of the stalking process.

Simple Is Better

"I think implementation is the key in everything. Implementation is more important than the trade idea behind it."

~ Colm O'Shea

Decisiveness is critical when it comes to your entry. In a fast-moving market, or if you are trading with the trend, you need to be ready to pull the trigger or else you could miss out on the opportunity. A confusing and complex entry approach is to be avoided. You don't need five indicators on a chart to all line up perfectly to time your buy. Instead, a simple breakout or limit order on a key level may be all you need.

With entries, simple is very much better!

STALK ON A LOWER TIMEFRAME TO IMPROVE THE RISK/REWARD

"Stalking means making sure the odds are even more in your favor by paying attention to the smallest time-frame possible for you."

~ Van Tharp

The main goals of a patiently stalked entry are to improve the risk/reward on the trade. To do this, you move to a lower timeframe, as it allows you to time your entry so that you can tighten your stop-loss. If you have a tighter stop-loss, you can take a larger position with the same number of dollars risked, meaning your profit on the position can be much greater or your risk much less.

If you had a set-up that gave you the potential to make 300 pips, with a risk of 100 pips, you would have a risk/reward ratio of 1:3. If, during your process of stalking an entry, you were able to get into the trade with a risk of only 50 pips, then you would have a potential risk/reward on the trade of 1:6.

On the weekly chart of the EUR/USD, we have a double top formation of resistance, signaling a change in trend. If our profit target is on the next level of support, we have a risk/reward ratio of 1:1.06, which is not great.

If instead we stalk an entry on the 4-hour chart, we can enter the trade with a significantly improved risk reward ratio of 1:3.6.

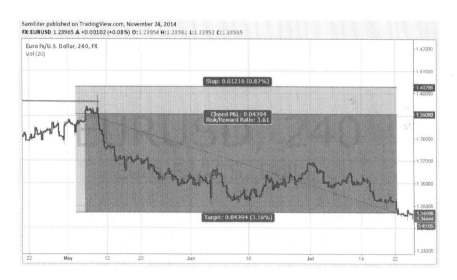

DO NOTHING UNLESS THERE IS SOMETHING TO DO

"I just wait until there is money lying around the corner, and all I have to do is go over there and pick it up. I do nothing in the meantime."

~ James Rogers

Many traders don't trade to win. They trade to get something else that they want from the markets. So instead of patiently stalking an entry, they feel the need to always be playing. But you can't rush the markets. If you try to force a position, it's pretty much guaranteed to come back and bite you. If you don't know what's going on, and if you don't have a superior risk/reward trade lined up, then you should not be trading. Simple as that.

If you have made a profit, there is no need to go out and place a new trade in a rush of overconfidence. A new opportunity will come if you give it time. If you have a losing trade, you don't need to do something to make it back—in fact, that is the worst thing you can do. Revenge trading is not a fruitful exercise. Get comfortable with "doing nothing". Make sure you center yourself after a winner or a loser, and only place a trade if you have a great deal of conviction in its success. A good trade should feel as if you are "shooting fish in a barrel", not as if you are taking a punt or hoping it will go your way.

IS THERE A FUNDAMENTAL CATALYST?

"You always need a catalyst to make big things happen."

~ James Rogers

When you assess an entry, it is good to check if there is a fundamental catalyst that is coinciding with the entry point. For example, if the price is breaking out, is it because of a surprising result from some economic news that has the potential to move the currency farther?

If there is a good fundamental catalyst, then it can improve the probability of your entry's success. You may even want to increase the position size on trades that have strong fundamental reasons for the entry.

IMPLEMENTATION PLAN

The way you implement your trade is directly related to how you manage your trade. For example, you may enter 50% at market with a wide stop and then the other 50% on a limit. Once the limit is triggered, you may choose to take all or part of the limit off once it gets back near your original entry. Conversely, you may decide to go all in at market with a tight stop. Obviously, this changes the way you manage the trade. When you implement your trade, you should consider which of the following entry methods you should use:

- 100% at market
- 50% at market and 50% on a limit
- Limit only
- Stop only

SPECIFIC ENTRIES THAT YOU CAN USE TODAY

"I developed and synthesized a number of indicators that I used to determine when the market was at a lower risk entry point."

~ Marty Schwartz

Here is a collection of entries you can use for your trading system. These can be used both on the original timeframe of the trade (on the weekly chart of a weekly set-up for example) or they can be used on a lower timeframe, so you can be very precise in your entry. After we cover these entries, we will discuss further the decision-making process and how entries fit into your overall trading approach.

CANDLESTICK PATTERNS

"I let the market tell me where it is going."

~ Mark Weinstein

Candlestick patterns can be excellent representations of the short term buying and selling pressure in the market and can be used to time entries. There are a lot of candlestick patterns and formations, but for our purposes, we will look at two. Just remember, they only tend to work well if they are used in conjunction with a damn good set-up, such as a key level.

The first pattern is known by a few names, such as "hammer", but we will call it a pin candle. To see this pattern, you will need to switch your chart to a candlestick chart. A pin candle occurs when there is a sharp reversal of the price within a time period, and it is a sign that the price is about to change direction and reverse. Here is an example of what a pin candle looks like:

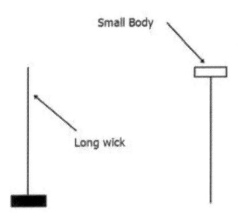

As you can see, the candle has a small body and a long tail or "wick". You would enter into a trade in the direction of the market—especially if there is a fundamental reason for doing so.

The next candlestick pattern that is of interest is called a bullish or bearish engulfing candlestick pattern. This pattern is prevalent at market reversals and during trends. Here are examples of bullish and bearish engulfing candles.

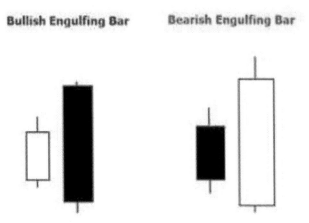

The key in each case is that the second candle in the pattern is larger than the first. The second candle should "engulf" the first candle. If you get a bullish engulfing, it is a sign to buy. If you get a bearish engulfing, it is a signal to sell. Here you can see the candlestick entry in action in the GBP/USD.

Note: There are a lot more candlestick patterns that can be used. For more information, look up Steve Nison's books.

TREND BREAKOUTS AFTER CONSOLIDATION

A breakout from consolidation entry is used when an existing trend pauses and consolidates for a period of sideways movement before the trend resumes. Ideally, what you want to do is look for a consolidation set-up, and then move to a lower chart to stalk the entry. The entry occurs when the price breaks out and closes above the range. With this entry, you should generally have a tight stop-loss, as price will either break out and continue in that direction or fall back within the range quickly.

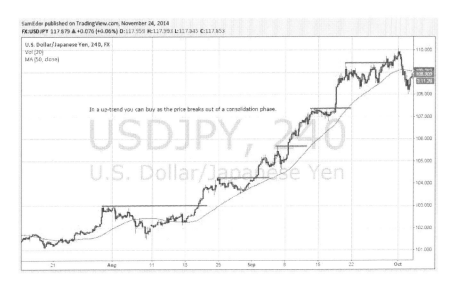

LOW-VOLATILITY BREAKOUTS

"Charts are extremely important."

~ Joe Vidich

Perhaps my favorite type of entry, the low-volatility breakout, is the epitome of the low risk/high reward trade idea. When prices compress into a tight range, they can expand rapidly into a strong directional move. To stalk this entry, I use the Bollinger Bands. Simply wait for bands to compress, and then take a position once the price breaks out.

I predominately use these entries in three circumstances.

- Once a trend has broken out, I look for periods of low volatility on a lower timeframe, and trade the breakout in the direction of the trend.

- I look for periods of low volatility off support or resistance levels to stalk reversals

- If I am day trading, I look for periods of low volatility leading into the London open, and look to trade a breakout from the range.

Here is an example of a low-volatility breakout on the EUR/AUD.

MOVING AVERAGE CROSSOVER

"I always check my charts and the moving averages before I take a position. Is the price above or below the moving average? That works better than any other tool I have. I try not to go against the moving averages [as] it's self-destructive."

~ Marty Schwartz

It's very easy to identify a moving average crossover, which is a big plus for using them as entries. You can also vary the speed of the moving average to suit your objectives. The way a moving average works is to identify the strength of the trend. Once the trend reaches a certain velocity, the faster-moving average will cross over the slower one, which gives us a signal to take a position. This means you are always buying or selling with the trend. A moving average crossover can also work as a counter-trend entry. If the price bounces off a support or resistance level, and the moving averages cross, it could be a good time to enter.

I like to use a three-period moving average, combined with a seven-period moving average. Once the three-period moving average crosses over the seven-period moving average, it provides an entry signal. I will also displace the shorter moving average by one period forward in time to make it easier for live trading.

Here is an example of moving average crossovers on GBP/USD.

How to Plan Your Trade & Trade Your Plan

Before moving on from entries, it's important to elaborate on the decision-making process around selecting entries. Good traders don't take every entry they see. Rather, they carefully plan ahead, and stalk a limited number of opportunities at a time. Seeing an entry candle does not mean you should automatically jump on it! This is crucial to internalize. If you find that trades pop up on you unawares, then lack of planning the trade and trading the plan is likely the issue.

Making Good Trading Decisions

The goal of planning your trades is so that, in the heat of the moment, you'll still be able to make good decisions. Carefully thought-out trades tend to work much better than ones taken on a whim in the fires of battle. If you fail to plan, all of your trades will end up as part of a scattergun approach that blows a big hole in your trading account.

The modern Forex trader is not a bank trader, absorbing multiple data inputs and placing dozens of trades based on an innate understanding of the markets. That era has ended. Now, a more systematic approach is required—one based around planning.

Don't Confuse Stalking with Planning, or Planning with Having a Trading Plan

Poor trading comes from poor processes. Whether or not you succeed as a trader doesn't hinge on your ability to recognize patterns; that's the easy part. Rather, your success (or lack thereof) depends on how effectively you can eliminate mistakes and promote good, overall decision making.

Erroneous trading often starts with a confused approach to planning (conducting market analysis) and stalking opportunities. **Planning your trades is a separate activity to executing your trades**. Your trade planning is also separate from your trading/system plan.

131

If it sounds confusing, it doesn't have to be. Essentially, you plan your system based on your model of the market. Then you plan, stalk entries, and manage your trades based on your system. It's all very linear and logical. The following diagram illustrates the distinction.

Decision making process

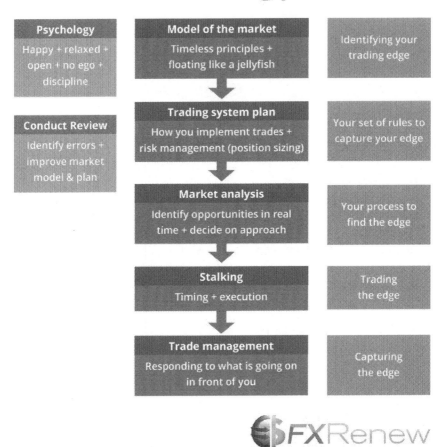

Your market model is the big-picture overview of how the market works. It is where you step back and identify opportunities with an edge. Your trading plan is where your position-sizing and trade-implementation rules are written down. These are both done prior to placing your trade in the planning phase. They are your preliminary work, so to speak, providing an overarching framework.

Next, you conduct market analysis to identify where your edge is appearing. Once you identify your edge in real-time, you assess how to best trade it. Then…it is time to be patient. Like a hunter stalking your prey, you wait for the optimal moment to enter the trade. Whereas your market model and trading plan are more general, you're now looking for the best risk/reward ratio possible for this specific trade.

These processes are then overlaid with your mental strategies, so you remain open to the opportunities and changes in the market and are better able to eliminate mistakes. Finally, after the trade, you conduct a review. With this information, you upgrade your market model, and improve your trading plan.

PUTTING IT INTO PRACTICE

The key to trading your plan is to treat market analysis as a separate phase, outside of your trading time. Schedule a time where you look for a set number of opportunities with very specific criteria. This is an important step, as you are not looking to trade every set-up or every candle pattern you come across. Rather, you are targeting a limited number of trading opportunities in order to achieve your return goals.

This could be one per day or one per week, for example. The exact number should be determined during your trading system development when you set objectives. Once you scan the markets for viable set-ups, you then select those of most interest. If you are looking at placing one trade per day, you might narrow it down to one, two, or three set-ups you like. You then want to write down how you will trade those set-ups. This includes:

- Entry criteria
- Position size
- Stop-loss placement
- Profit targets
- Any other foreseeable exit conditions (how, when, and why to pull the ripcord)

You should know exactly where you will enter, how much you will trade, where you will exit with a loss, and how you plan to farm profits. This should not be made up on the spot; it comes directly from the trading system plan—your overarching framework.

Next, you need to decide what to do if more than one of your entries is triggered. Do you take the first one, and cancel the rest, or is there one you would prefer to take, with the others as backup? You need to know exactly what to do here, or you will get confused and end up with sub-optimal trades. Remember…you are not trying to catch every move. It's okay to let some go by.

ONLY THEN MOVE ON TO STALKING YOUR TRADE

Wait for your exact pre-planned entry criteria to be fulfilled before entering a trade, and act decisively as soon as they are. At this point, it should all be quite simple as your entry has been triggered, and you have a plan for how you are going to trade it. It is just a matter of executing accurately. Failure in this area results in an execution gap. You can be a great analyst but a poor trader by failing to implement your trades in the correct manner or by acting indecisively.

After the trade is entered, you then need to observe the market, and respond appropriately to what is going on. This is where you run your trade management plan (more on this in coming chapters). If an exit condition occurs for any given trade, you simply follow the steps you have outlined in your analysis phase (again, based on your system trading plan). Anything else that happens, as far as you should be concerned, is just noise to be ignored.

AVOID BEING REACTIONARY

There may be times when you think you could or should have entered a trade or taken profit. But unless they are part of your plan, you should not act upon these impulses. Note down these situations, and assess them later on when the blood is not running so hot. The idea being that you can add to your market model and your wider trading plan later, once you have rigorously assessed any observations to make sure they are valid and worthy additions.

SIMPLICITY WILL HAVE ITS REWARDS

"Don't trade until an opportunity presents itself. Knowing when to stay out of the markets is as important as knowing when to be in them."

~ Mark Weinstein

One of the best ways to master the art of trading is to pick and choose a limited number of techniques first, and get to grips with them. Select one or two entries you like, and practice them. Be patient when you hunt for your entries, and keep them simple, too, so you can act decisively when the time comes.

How Your Stops Get Hunted and What to Do About It

"Whenever I enter a position, I have a predetermined stop. That is the only way I can sleep. I know when I am getting out before I get in."

~ Bruce Kovner

Have you ever had your stop hit at what turned out to be the low? Was it just bad luck? Or is there something more at play? Forex trading is a zero-sum game. One person's loss is another person's win. You can bet that the strong players with more information, more money, and the ability to move the market are out to get as much easy profit as they can. This means the retail players left holding the weak hand (i.e. with stop-losses) had better watch out.

But the dealers can be beat. By sidestepping traps and learning how to place your stop-loss in places that are difficult to hit, you could add significantly to your trading bottom line. The first step is to understand dealing ranges...

How Dealing Ranges Influence the Price

"The most important thing is to have a method of staying with your winners and getting rid of your losers."

~ Gary Beilfeldt

Dealing ranges drive market behavior. A dealing range is simply a high and a low for a trading session or a time period, such as a day, a week, or a month. Dealers use these levels to work out their orders and manage their positions. You can see examples of dealing ranges on the 15-minute chart of the EUR/USD here:

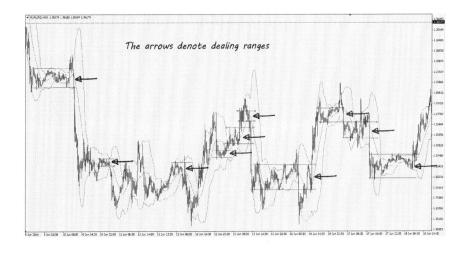

The arrows denote dealing ranges

Dealing ranges exist on multiple timeframes. You can see the dealing ranges here on the 4-hour chart:

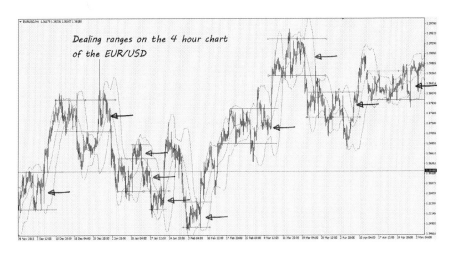

Dealing ranges on the 4 hour chart of the EUR/USD

Dealing ranges are imprecise. The edges of the range are often pierced, and the levels the dealers use for reference are fluid. You will notice that an old dealing range will often form the basis for a new dealing range; in other words, they act as support and resistance levels. This is a type of market structure that is tradable and can provide you with an edge. In the following chart, you can see old ranges are used as reference points for new ranges.

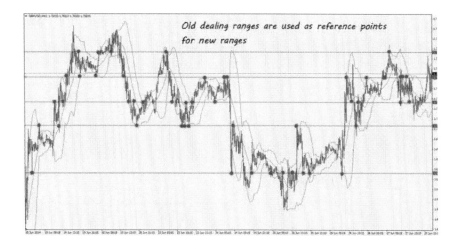

Traders who are taught to put their stops behind support and resistance levels will often put their stop-loss orders behind dealing ranges. But the problem for these traders is that their stops then become a target for those who want to be on the other side of the trade at that price. This is true of any major level. You can see this quite clearly on most Forex charts.

On the following chart, I have marked with red dots where a move has taken out stops before reversing above or below either the dealing range or a support and resistance level.

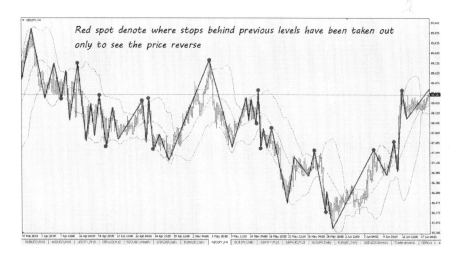

You can see how often your stops would be taken out if you were not careful about your entry or where your stop-loss was placed. So the solution is simple: Widen your stops, and don't put them so close to the edge of the dealing range...? Not always. There are other factors to consider first.

TIGHT STOPS IMPROVE THE RISK-TO-REWARD RATIO OF YOUR TRADES

There is a problem with widening your stops. A wider stop means that when you do lose, you lose more. Also, consider that you may decide to trade less in total in order to compensate for a wider stop. In this case, your winners would win you less. Both of these factors will have a negative impact on the risk/reward ratio of your trades. When you do win, you will make less compared to your losses than if you had a tighter stop. On the flipside of the coin, it could mean you will have more winning trades to compensate for the smaller wins. By widening your stop, your win percentage improves.

WIDE STOPS CAN IMPROVE THE QUALITY OF YOUR SYSTEM

"Place your stops at a point that, if reached, will reasonably indicate that the trade is wrong, not at a point determined primarily by the maximum dollar amount you are willing to lose."

~ Bruce Kovner

If you have a wide stop, you will, in general:

- Improve your winning percentage
- Increase your flexibility when managing your trade

If your stop is farther from the market, it gives you more latitude on your entry. If you get the general direction right but not the exact timing, a wide stop will allow the market to move against you a little before settling in your general direction. This means you will, on average, have more winning trades than if you have a tight stop.

In addition, if your stop is wider, you will have more opportunity to manage your trade and get out with a loss that is smaller than 1R. For example, you might experience a reversal right on entry and choose to get out with a small 0.2R loss. If your stop-loss was tighter, then you might have ended up with a 0.5R loss or even a 1R loss.

For the savvy trader, having more winning trades and losses that are smaller than 1R could significantly increase the quality of their trading system. If you have a higher-quality trading system, then your position-sizing model can allow you to trade at a larger size, compensating for the decreased risk/reward ratio on your trade.

STOP-LOSSES ARE INEXTRICABLY LINKED TO YOUR ENTRY STRATEGY AND TRADE OBJECTIVES

"I have a mental stop. If it hits that number I am out no matter what."

~ Paul Tudor Jones

Your stop-loss should be a logical extension of your entry strategy and the objectives you have for the trade. For example, if you are a trend follower, looking to catch a breakout, you might have a tight stop-loss that you expect to get hit more often than not. Or if your goal were to have a 3:1 risk/reward ratio on your trade, you would have a tighter stop than if you were going for 1:1. Logically choose a stop that fits holistically into your trading strategy.

PSYCHOLOGY AND STOP-LOSSES

Losses can be difficult to take, as traders like to be "right" and would prefer to avoid taking losses. The trick is not to associate loss with failure. Instead, it's important to see a loss as a "cost of doing business"—in other words, the results of any one trade don't matter.

Rather, it is the distribution of outcomes over a series of trades that matters. You will win some and lose some, and it is what you end up with over time that is important, not the results of any individual trade.

Another psychological challenge with stop-losses is that the more losses you have in a row, the less confidence you may have in your system. The next trade after a big loser will be more difficult to take, even if you know over the long run that your system performs profitably. So make sure that when developing your stop-loss strategy, you consider your ability to continue to execute your system even after a series of losses. If your stop-losses are too tight, then, even if you do have the occasional big winning trade, you might find the strategy too challenging to trade without making critical errors.

MARKET TYPES AND STOP-LOSSES

As the market types shift and change, so should your approach to the market. This goes for stop-losses, too. Consider whether your stop-loss placement is suited to the current market type. In addition, be prepared to change your strategy for your stop-loss if the market type changes during a trade.

A NOTE ON VOLATILE MARKET TYPES

Common wisdom espouses that during a volatile market type, you should widen your stop-loss. I am of a different opinion. If the market type becomes volatile, you want to tighten your stop-loss. The markets have just gotten a whole lot hairier, and you don't want to give the market room to move against you. You will need to prepare to be stopped out more often in this market type. However, by having tight stops, you will have the opportunity for some quick profits when things do go your way.

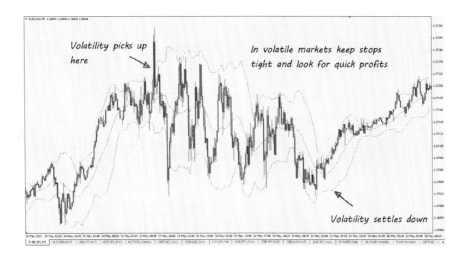

Volatility picks up here

In volatile markets keep stops tight and look for quick profits

Volatility settles down

Superior Options for Stop-Loss Placement

"When I am wrong the only instinct I have is to get out."

~ Michael Platt

Your main considerations for stop-loss placement are:

- The dealing ranges
- The risk/reward ratio
- Your entry and trade objectives
- The market type
- When your idea is proven wrong.

Understanding this, here are some different strategies for placing stops that can help to improve the profitability of your trades.

Support and Resistance Stop-loss

The classic place for Forex traders to place stops is behind support and resistance levels. Just be aware of the stop-hunting intentions of those participants who can move the market. You could put your stop

10-25 pips or 0.25-0.5% beyond the level, which will help you to avoid some of the whipsaws, but remember, this will impact the risk/reward on the trade.

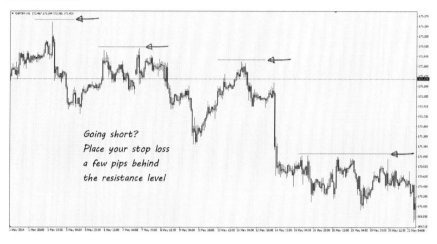

SHAKE-OUT STOP-LOSS

Wait until after the stops have been hunted and the price has reversed before you enter. Then place your stop-loss either directly behind the support or resistance level—or even slightly inside it—to improve the risk/reward on the trade. On the following chart, you can see how once the stops have been taken out (the thin red line), it is safe to place your own stop-loss (the thick red line).

Indicator Stop-loss

Indicator stop-losses can be quite useful for three reasons: They give you a consistent place to put your stop that requires little discretion. They are (or should be!) relevant to your entry and trade objectives. The stop will not be in the usual place that other market participants will be targeting. For example, you could put your stop-loss on the blue (100 period) moving average on the 15-minute chart of the USD/JPY when you enter short on this moving-average crossover strategy.

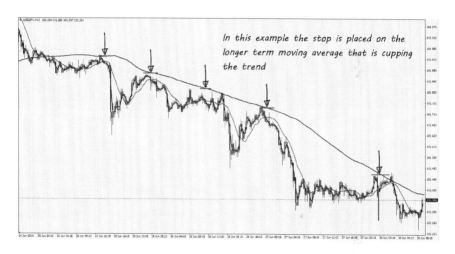

In this example the stop is placed on the longer term moving average that is cupping the trend

The "Midair" Stop-loss

To avoid being "stop-hunted", a mid-air stop is just the ticket. Mid-air stops are set far enough away from the edge of the range to make it difficult for it to be hit. In addition, as your stop is likely to be on its own and not grouped with a bunch of others, there will be little point in others going for it, anyway. Mid-air stops work best when trading directly off support and resistance levels. You simply place your stop far enough away from the dealing range that it will look like it is hanging in mid-air, away from the action.

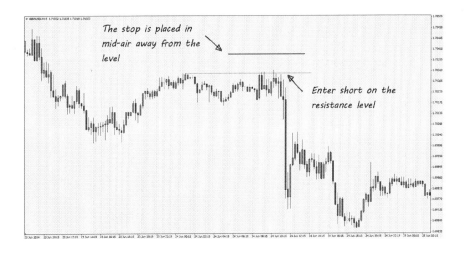

The stop is placed in mid-air away from the level

Enter short on the resistance level

A SPECIAL NOTE ON BREAKEVEN STOPS

"Getting out sometimes right before the [currency pair] turns is the price you pay to keep your losses under control."

~ Joe Vidich

There are both pros and cons for breakeven stops. On the one hand, a breakeven stop is a powerful psychological tool. It ensures your winning trades don't turn into losing ones. This means your winning percentage will increase, which can make it psychologically easier to follow your system and trade mistake free.

On the other hand, if you move your stop-loss to breakeven, you may end up putting your stop in an illogical place that the dealers can easily go for. In my experience, this can mean that although you have less losing trades, you will actually make less overall. The winning trades you miss out on will reduce the profitability of your system over time. Be careful not to trail your stop too quickly to breakeven, and get prematurely knocked out of otherwise profitable trades.

So What to Do Next?

"Simplicity is the ultimate sophistication."

~Leonardo da Vinci

Now it becomes a simple matter of testing. Try adjusting the following combination to see what suits your system:

- The risk/reward ratio by tightening and widening stops
- The stop-loss method.

Always think about the dealing ranges. Keep in mind where the market is likely to move to next, and avoid putting your stop in places that are easy to hit. Remember, your loss is their gain.

How to Trade What's in Front of You with a Complex Exit Strategy

"Don't worry about what the markets are going to do, worry about what you are going to do in response to the market."

~ Michael Carr

After you get into your trade, different things happen. Very rarely does your trade go in a straight line to your profit objective. So if you only have one tool in your toolbox, you are going to struggle to react effectively to what is happening in front of you. If you only have a hammer, everything is going look like a nail, even when your trade is screaming for a screwdriver or a measuring tape.

Instead, pack your toolbox full of different tools for different scenarios. That way, when the moment calls for it, you can appropriately make the right decisions about when to stay in your trade and when to exit based on what the market is doing at the time. In general, you will want to have the following types of exits at your disposal:

- An exit rule if the trade reaches your profit objective
- An exit rule in case of reversal right after entry
- An exit rule for an intra-trade drawdown
- An exit rule if the trade moves steadily in your favor and then reverses
- An exit rule for a fast-moving market in your favor
- An exit rule for a fast-moving market against you
- An exit rule for once the price gets close to your profit objective and starts to fall away
- An exit rule for chart patterns that signal reversals
- An exit rule if fundamental or sentiment conditions change.

SIMPLE ENTRIES VS. COMPLEX EXITS

In chapter 10, we learned that your actual rule for getting into the trade should be simple. Complexity is the enemy of decisiveness. Why, then, am I saying you should have a complex exit strategy?

Each component of your exit strategy on its own is quite simple, yet when combined, they form a complex exit strategy. Contrary to the popular wisdom that a simple trading plan is better, exits need to be able to cater to many different circumstances. Ideally, you want to have a set of clear rules that will allow you to manage risk and protect your profits, depending on what the market does.

THE MARKET IS GOING TO FORCE YOU TO MAKE DECISIONS

Throughout your trade, the market is going to throw you all sorts of different scenarios. It is going to force you to make decisions about what to do constantly. Often, it will be best to sit tight and do nothing, but there will be times when you should take action. At each of these "decision points", your complex exit strategy comes into play.

You will need to assess the current market, and apply the right tool for the job to manage your trade properly. A decision point could arise because of market action, or it could arise because a pre-planned price was hit. A reversal pattern could form, or the price could reverse a number of R-multiples, and you need to decide if you are going to stay in the trade, or if it's time to exit or reduce your position size. Be aware that these decision points are going to happen, and be ready to act when they do. Trading what's in front of you is all about being prepared.

Learn to Expect What Comes Next, and Play the Probabilities

"Your job is to follow the system. If the system does something that results in losses. That's just an expected part of the system. Your Judgement might be on the line over the performance of the entire system, but there is no sense in which your judgement is on the line on any single trade."

~ William Eckhardt

In developing your complex exit strategy, it is important to understand market types. If you know what market type the currency pair is in, then you can predict what might follow. For example, a bull normal market will often transition to a bull volatile and then a volatile sideways phase before falling into a bear market. If you know this is the probable outcome, you can plan your exits accordingly.

Developing Your Complex Exit Strategy

"I let the market dictate to me how I should be trading, not my macro views of what I think the market will do."

~ Larry Benedict

As you develop your trading system, you will need to build a set of exit rules that fit you and the other components of your trading plan (such as your entry and trading timeframe). Let's look now at each of the specific exits you will want to be able to call on.

Profit Objective

"I always take money off the table when it's in my favor. Always, always, always."

~ Jimmy Balodimas

When your trade hits your profit objective, you have a number of options:

- Close the position manually

- Have a set profit target to automatically close the position

- Tighten the stop-loss, and let the position run

- Take off some of the position, and let the rest run

- Make no changes, and continue in the trade

- Wait for a reversal signal.

It is a balance between letting your profits run and locking in your gains. What you do here will very much depend on your trading style and personality.

TECHNIQUES

Profit objectives serve as guides for your trade. Your profit objective does not have to be a fixed price, though it can be helpful to have a predefined point when you will exit. If you don't have a profit objective—for instance, if you are following a trend—then make sure your trading decisions reflect that.

A useful profit objective can be a resistance level such as an old high, because the chance of the price reversing increases once it hits this level, as profit taking often occurs. You could also use a Fibonacci level or pivot point. The important thing is to have a logical place to exit.

INTRA-TRADE DRAWDOWN

"Never sell the strongest markets until they fail."

~ Scott Ramsey

One of the cardinal sins amateur traders commit is letting winning trades turn into losing trades. To stop this scenario from happening, you can apply a maximum intra-trade drawdown rule, or amount you are willing to give back in order to achieve further gains.

TECHNIQUES

Generally, you would select a maximum R-multiple you are willing to give back. For example, if you have a 5R winner, you may institute a trailing stop of 2R or 3R, so you lock in some of your profits. If you are going for a large profit objective, you may need to be prepared to give back more R multiples than if you are going for a short profit objective.

Another method is to trail the stop two or three bars behind the current price in the direction of your trade. This serves to protect profit, while at the same time allowing the stop to be placed in a position that is "market-based" rather than an arbitrary R-multiple.

REVERSAL RIGHT AFTER ENTRY

"You have to always be pragmatic enough to move with the market."

~ Martin Taylor

You have patiently waited for your entry and seemingly timed it to perfection, but as soon as you enter, the market forms a reversal signal. If this happens to you, then you are faced with a decision point. Do you now exit the position, lighten it, or leave it, and see what happens? Generally, it can be a good idea to trust what you are seeing, and at least take some off the table.

TECHNIQUES

There are several chart patterns that indicate that the price has reversed right after entry. These could be:

- A candlestick or bar formation

- A candlestick or bar formation on a different time-frame chart

- A double top or double bottom

- Three consecutive bars or candles in the opposite direction to your trade

- A close below the resistance level for a long trade or above support for a short trade.

If you get one of these immediately after your entry, then it can be worth closing out early, as it may be a sign that the breakout has failed, or the edge has disappeared.

THE TRADE MOVES STEADILY IN YOUR FAVOR AND THEN REVERSES

Sometimes your trade will enter a nice, efficient phase, where it steadily moves in your direction. It is easy to continue to hold the position during this period, but what do you do when the market starts to reverse?

Do you exit the trade immediately, or do you decide to hang on until the trend re-establishes itself? It is important to consider your objectives for the trade when you make this decision. If you have a long-term objective, you will need to leave room for the trade to breathe.

TECHNIQUES

Technical indicators such as Bollinger Bands and Moving Averages can serve as trailing stops. As a general rule, the longer the timeframe of the indicators you use to manage intra-trade drawdowns, the larger the drawdowns will be (but you will have a greater chance of having a large win).

VOLATILE, FAST-MOVING MARKETS IN YOUR FAVOR

"The sharpness of the move indicates that volatility has just increased; hence, even a windfall profit might dissipate rapidly."

~ *William Eckhart*

"One of my rules was to get out when the volatility and momentum become absolutely insane."

~ *Michael Marcus*

Fast-moving markets can rapidly reverse and chew through the profits you have made. It's best to lock profits in, and wait for a re-entry. Sometimes, this will mean you miss out on a move as you get stopped out, but more often than not, it will save your skin.

TECHNIQUES

There are a few techniques you can use to retain your profits in a fast-moving market.

- Tighten your stop to 0.5 – 1.5R from the current price
- Wait for a cross of a short-term moving average, such as the 3-period EMA displaced by 3 periods
- Go to a lower timeframe chart to manage the trade
- Look for a chart-pattern reversal

If the price is trading outside the outer Bollinger Bands, wait for the first close back inside.

Finding the right one (or combination) that fits you will take a little bit of live-trading experience. You need to react quickly when you encounter this scenario, so be sure to use a rule that is congruent with your trading style.

VOLATILE, FAST-MOVING MARKETS MOVING AGAINST YOU

One of the more uncomfortable scenarios to face is when the market moves suddenly against you. This can happen when there is unexpected news, a global macro-event, or a sudden change in supply and demand.

TECHNIQUES

If this happens, you have a couple of choices, depending on your trading style and your view of the strength of the reason for the drop. You could get out immediately, and take the loss, or you could wait, and hope the position rebounds in your favor. This can be a very challenging decision to make, but, whatever you do, keep risk management at the top of your mind.

If you find yourself staying in a trade, desperately hoping it will recover, then you are probably better off cutting your losses and exiting the position. One compromise when faced with this scenario is to move your stop up tightly below the current price. If it recovers, then you will benefit, but any further losses are strictly limited.

THE PRICE GETS CLOSE TO YOUR PROFIT OBJECTIVE AND STARTS TO FALL AWAY

An all-too-common occurrence for a trader is to have their trade going almost to the profit target, not quite hitting it, and then falling all the way down to the stop-loss. This is the classic "turning a winner into a loser" trap. Not only does this cost the trader profits, it can be frustrating and psychologically damaging in the long run.

Techniques

A remedy for this is to make sure your risk/reward ratio during a trade is never worse than 1:1. For example, if the currency price is 10 pips away from your profit target, and your stop-loss is 50 pips in the opposite direction, you would have a terrible risk/reward of 1:5. That is, you are risking 50 pips in order to make an additional 10. In this case, you would tighten your stop to within 10 pips of the current price, dynamically re-establishing the 1:1 risk/reward ratio. This exit has the effect of tightening your stop once you get close to your profit target. Note that it can be impractical to use this at all times, so I normally put this rule into play once the price gets to within striking distance of the original target.

Chart Pattern Reversals

Often, a chart pattern will indicate to you that the price is about to reverse, and now is the time to act to protect your profits. But be careful, as some reversals are not as strong as others, and you don't want to be cutting your profits short by exiting on weak signals.

It will be tempting to close your trades early if you don't have this aspect of your exit strategy down pat. If you do see a reversal and you are unsure if you should close your position or not, then you can always scale out or move your stop higher.

Techniques

There are plenty of chart-pattern reversals that can occur throughout the trade.

- Candlestick and bar patterns
- Classical chart pattern, such as flags, pennants, and wedges
- Double tops and bottoms.

The important thing is to know how to identify them and to have a plan on how to react to them when they do occur. For shorter-term reversal patterns, such as candlesticks, you can wait for them to happen in combination with support or resistance levels. Rather than exit at market, you can use these reversal patterns a sign to tighten your stop-loss instead of exiting straight away. This will give you a little time to reassess, and check that you have not made a mistake in identifying the chart pattern.

FUNDAMENTAL OR SENTIMENT CONDITIONS CHANGE

If fundamental or sentiment conditions dictate that the trade no longer makes sense, then you can take profit. For example, if you experience a change in the news cycle from positive to negative, it can be a good time to exit your position. Say the market was ignoring bad news and continuing to push higher, then you would continue with the trade. But if the market starts to sell off during bad news suddenly, then you know something has changed, and it's time to get out. Similarly, there could be a macro-event or other news that could cause a change in the price movement of the currency pair you are trading.

If your assessment is that this is likely to continue, then you should close the trade.

KEEPING IS SIMPLE

For the newbie trader, this might seem like a lot of work, and it is. Therefore, it is important to make it easy on yourself when you first start to define your complex exit strategy. Firstly, you should make some choices about what to do when the price hits your profit objective. I would suggest tightening the stop and looking to let the position run, or setting a profit target.

Secondly, you want to have a maximum, intra-trade drawdown stop. I would suggest you use a 3R stop, so you will never let a trade go into a drawdown of greater than 3 times your initial risk after it is in profit.

Thirdly, you will want a stop for fast-moving markets. I would suggest that if you ever see the market rapidly take off in your favor, then implement a 0.5-1.5R trailing stop.

Next, you could investigate some stops based on chart-pattern reversals. Candlestick patterns work well for identifying these reversals, particularly in combination with support and resistance.

TRADE IN THE MOMENT WITH THE MARKET

"Don't think about what the market's going to do; you have absolutely no control over that. Think about what you are going to do if it gets there."

~ William Eckhart

By implementing a complex exit strategy, you will have the tools you need to be in the moment with the market, and trade what is in front of you. Putting together a set of exit rules is going to take some time, and that is okay. You can start by applying the "keeping it simple" rules above, and then add more rules to your plan over time.

Advanced Trade-Management Techniques

"It's not about being right; it's about making money."

~ Scott Ramsey

"I scale in and scale out of my positions, so that I can spread out my risk."

~Tony Saliba

It's the ultimate Forex traders' dream: Have a big position on a trade that goes your way, and get out with a large profit. With all the large moves in the Forex market, it should be easy, right? Turns out, it's not as simple as you might think. To manage risks on a large position, and then to get out with your profits before the market reverses, requires hard work—and lots of it. The good news is there is a technique to it. There is no need to put on a large trade and "hope like hell" it goes your way. Instead, you can use trade-management rules to build a position while limiting your risk and then to hold onto your profits when it comes time to exit.

This is one way you, as a retail trader, can grow your small account into a big one. Implementing trade-management techniques allows you to build a large, leveraged position while minimizing risk, which provides you with the opportunity for big profits.

These techniques involve:

- Scaling into a position
- Scaling out of a position
- Re-entering into a position
- Trading against a core position
- Building a risk-free position.

Advanced trade-management techniques work hand in hand with the complex exit strategies in chapter 12. This chapter and chapter 12 focuses on managing your position after the trade is placed. Your position-sizing model from chapter 7 is also inextricably linked to your trade-management techniques.

DON'T TRY TO BE 100% RIGHT WHEN YOU TRADE

"You have to trade at a size such that if you are not exactly right in your timing, you won't be blown out of your position. My approach is to build a larger size as the market is going my way. I don't put on a trade by saying "my god this is the level; the market is taking off right from here." I am definitely a scale-in type of trader. I do the same thing getting out of positions. I don't say, "fine I've made enough money. This is it I'm out." Instead I start to lighten up as I see the price action or fundamental changing."

~ Bill Lipschutz

"Don't try to be 100% right."

~ Joe Vidich

By using a series of structured entry and exit points throughout the trade, you don't have to be 100% right on your timing. You simply have to be right on your idea. Of course, if you are spot-on with your timing, it can be helpful, but it's not necessary to win big in the market.

Once you have an idea and the price action is in alignment with it, you can then start to develop your position. If you are right and price action continues to confirm your idea, you can continue to grow your position to a meaningful size. If you are in a position and you sense the market is about to turn, you can begin to lighten your position. If you are wrong and the market continues to be favorable, you still have skin in the game and can rebuild your trade; if you are right and the market turns, you can continue to lock in profits.

Contrast this with a single-position approach:

If you take a full-sized position and lose, then you will have lost the maximum amount. If you take all your profits in one go, and the market continues in your direction, you have broken one of the cardinal rules of trading and cut your profits short.

In particular, this scaling method is suited to the retail trader. It allows you to focus more on your position sizing and risk management, which is one of your edges over larger market participants, and less on being right on the particular timing, which is a challenging skill to master.

IMPLEMENTATION IS MORE IMPORTANT THAN THE TRADE IDEA ITSELF

"Having a beautiful idea does not get you very far if you don't do it the right way."

~ Colm O'Shea

It's not about being right; it's about how much you make when you are right. Have you ever picked a trade perfectly and then not done anything about it or taken only a small position, and all the while the market did exactly what you thought it would? Your problem was implementation.

Many of the market wizards talk about how implementation of the trade idea they have developed is more important than the trade itself. If you have a good idea but fail to capitalize on it or to effectively manage your risks, then the idea itself is pretty worthless.

The concept behind advanced trade-management techniques is to implement trade ideas skillfully, based on your trading objectives. When you enter into a position, plan ahead on how you are going to generate the most profit you can from it. Ask yourself some questions:

- What is the current market type, and how can you best build a position in this market type?

- Do you need to scale into the position quickly, as you expect it to get away from you? Or can you take your time to build the position?

- Are there any points along the way to your profit objective that you want to take profit and then re-enter?

- Where are the likely opportunities to trade against or hedge your core position?

- Is there a way to build a risk-free position if the price chops around near the entry for a while?

- How will you manage risk to both your starting capital and profits gained during the trade?

- With experience you will be able to implement your trade in a very advanced manner.

SCALING IN WITH LOW-RISK ENTRY POINTS

"The way to build long-term returns is through preservation of capital and home runs. You can be far more aggressive when you are making a good profit... The way to attain truly superior long-term returns is to grind out until you are up 30 or 40 percent and then if you have the convictions, to go for a 100% year. If you can put together a few near 100% years and avoid down years, you can achieve really out-standing long-term returns."

~ Stanley Druckenmiller

While there are a number of ways to profit from the currency market, one way is to take a big position and ride it hard. If the market goes for you and you are highly leveraged in the right direction, your profits can be grand. This is the goal of scaling in...to build a large position so if the market moves in your favor, it will generate a significant profit.

Scaling in to a position is when you place a number of trades over time and at different prices with the goal of building a larger position. By taking a small initial position—one that causes a negligible loss if it goes against you—then you are protecting your core capital. As the trade goes for you, you can add positions, and you have the profit from the original position to cushion you from any fall in the price of your new positions, which keeps your overall risk on the account at a manageable level while at the same time keeping you in the running for massive profits.

To do this, you would generally keep your initial position as only a small percentage of your maximum position size. For example, if you have a maximum trade size of $300,000, then your first position might be only $100,000 (depending on your conviction on the trade).

You would then continue to add trades until you reach your maximum position size. For example, you could add trades until they reach your maximum position size of $300,000. You could do this by adding to your position three to five times as the price moves in your direction for example.

STALKING SCALE-IN POINTS

You can develop many different formulas for scaling in to trades, but one of the best ways to do it is to stalk low-risk, scale-in points as you would low-risk entry points.

For example, if the price breaks though key levels, if you get a pull-back and reversal candle in the direction of your trade, or if you get some news that is supportive of your position, then you can add additional positions to the trade.

There is no need to be complicated about when you scale in; the most important thing is to have a plan and to follow it.

COMBINING YOUR POSITION, OR USING MULTIPLE STOP-LOSSES

As you scale in to positions, you have some choices to make about where to place your stop-loss. You can:

- Treat each new position as an individual position with its own stop-loss.

- Manage the risk on all positions together with one combined stop-loss.

If you treat each position separately, you may end up being stopped out on some of your scale-in entry points, but you will not suffer such wild swings of your equity throughout the trade. Plus, you could end up still holding your original position when you would have been stopped out of it if you were combining the risk management together.

Managing the risk together with one stop-loss is the more aggressive option, as it will mean you will generally end up with a larger position if the trend does go your way. For example, you might move the stop-loss so that, at any stage, you are risking no more than 2% of your account on the entire position.

SCALING OUT OF A POSITION

"Hopefully I spend the rest of the day enjoying positions that are going in my direction. If they are going in my direction I have a game plan for getting out."

~ *Paul Tudor Jones*

"If it re-enters its base I have a rule to cut at least 50% of the position."

~ *David Ryan*

Once you have carefully crafted your large position using a scale-in methodology, you may not want exiting out of it to be an all or nothing decision.

Again, it comes down to your psychology. If there is a tremendous pressure to be "right" about where you exit, then you are highly likely to make mistakes, and cut your profits short or "hold on and hope". Instead, if you have a series of exit rules and you use them to appropriately scale out of parts of your trade, you don't have to be perfect on your timing to farm profits from the market. This allows you to lock in profit when the probabilities are on your side, while at the same time keeping money in the market in case it really goes for you. You can see on the chart below that you often get the opportunity take off a percentage of your position when the market gives signs it is reversing.

RE-ENTERING INTO A POSITION

Sometimes, you exit a position based on market action, and you want to get straight back in. At other times, you might take profit, and look to re-establish your position later. To do this, you can use a re-entry methodology.

Re-entries are used in two circumstances:

- When you close the entire position.

- When you close part of the position.

If your stop-loss or trailing stop for your position is hit, then you will be closing your entire position, but often stops get hit, and the market reverses in your favor. In this case, you can choose to either re-enter the whole position or to start to scale back in to the original position.

When you take profit, you might look to re-establish part or all of your position at a better price. As the market does not always go in a straight line to your objective, this strategy of selling at key levels and waiting for a pullback can work very well. In fact, you will find a lot of "old dog" traders who use this as their primary strategy.

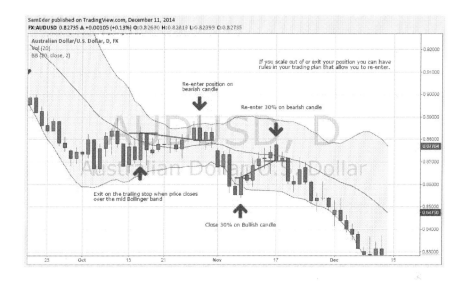

TRADING AGAINST AND HEDGING THE CORE POSITION

Trading against or hedging a core position is really about your trader mindset.

When it comes down to it, exiting part of your position has the same real effect as trading against or hedging a position. If you are short 10 lots and you buy 3 lots, then you are net 7 lots short, no matter if you have established a new position, closed some of your original position, or placed the trade as a hedge. Confused? Don't worry too much: it's a tricky concept to grasp (and I did call this chapter "advanced" trade-management techniques).

What you really need to know is that, for some traders, opening a trade in the opposite direction to their core position can be a good thing. Much of it is about comfort and attention. If you have a big cushion of profits, it should give you confidence. If you have a large winning position, you are likely following the currency pair very closely and will have developed a strong sense of its ebb and flow. This means you could be very good at picking spots when it's going to go against you. So why not place a trade?

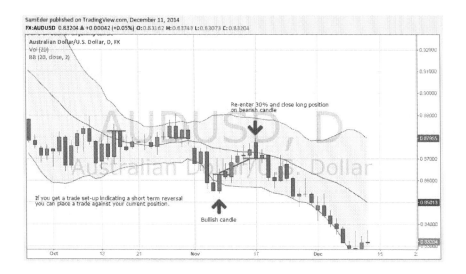

There is another significant benefit of trading against the core position. If you generate profits from the trade, you can then use them to add more size to the original position. This is one way of building a very large position for a trade.

HEDGING WITH CROSS RATES

Another tool you have at your disposal for managing your trades is the ability to hedge your core position with a cross rate, thus converting your trade into a "synthetic position" in a different currency pair. You might do this to hedge against short-term weakness in the base currency of your trade or to benefit from temporary strength in another currency. For example, if you are short the AUD/USD for the long term but are wary of USD weakness over the short term, you could buy GBP/USD, which would give you a synthetic long GBP/AUD position. This means you would benefit if the GBP were stronger than the USD for the period of the hedge.

172

BUILDING A RISK-FREE POSITION

"I can get hit when I have been getting paid, but it's hard for me to get hit from a standing start. That is key."

~ Scott Ramsey

Imagine if you had a large position in a currency pair that would benefit you greatly if it goes your way but has little-to-no risk if it goes against you. Would be nice, wouldn't it? Building a risk-free position relies on the fact that markets don't always take off straight away in your direction. Instead, they often chop around a while before finally giving way to a trend.

If you have conviction that the currency pair is going to move in a certain direction, then you can start to place long and short trades within the choppy movement around your entry. For example, you might go long 3 lots and then short 3 lots then long 4 lots, etc. on each short-term reversal.

As you accumulate profits, you can start to trade a bigger size, offsetting your risk with the profits and with some luck, eventually getting to a point where your profits more than cover any risk you have on the trade—a risk-free position.

Market type identification is important here. If you have a view and the market type is sideways, you can then start to build your position. Once you get the move in your anticipated direction, then you can use the profits you have already generated from the sideways price action for your trade.

SamEder published on TradingView.com, December 11, 2014
FX:AUDUSD 0.83224 ▲ +0.00062 (+0.07%) O:0.83162 H:0.83743 L:0.83073 C:0.83224

TYING IT ALL TOGETHER

"As I continued to incorporate more "expert trader rules" my system became more compatible with my trading style."

~ *Ed Seykota*

You can see here how all the entry and exit points we have outlined in the lesson come together in a trade on the AUD/USD.

- You use the sideways market type to build a risk-free position.

- Once you get the breakout, you quickly scale in on the first part of the move.

- As the price starts to reverse, you take profits.

- Before adding the position back on as the original trend resumes.

- You trade against the core position before closing out as the trend resumes.

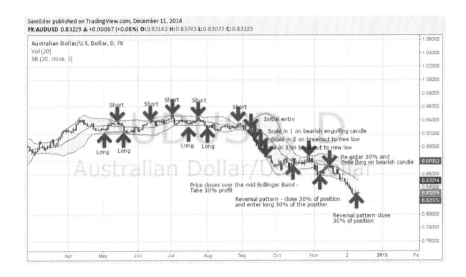

Of course, at some point, you are going to need to close the position completely. To do that, you would use your complex exit strategy from chapter 12.

TIME TO GET OUT YOUR TRADING PLAN

"You need to develop a plan of your strategies for various contingencies. By having thought out your objective and having a strategy for getting out in case the market trend changes, you greatly increase the potential for staying in your winning positions."

~ Gary Bielfeldt

dvanced trade management is a lucrative skill to master. To do it well, you need to be very clear in your objectives as well as in sync with the market. But you don't need to get it perfect. If you can do half as well as this example that I have used throughout this chapter, you will be in for some very healthy paydays.

Think about how you want to manage your trades, write it down in your trading plan, and make sure you follow it. Managing the large positions you will be able to build is going to take discipline, so having written rules is essential.

How to Run Your Trading Business Like a Hedge Fund

"Longevity is the key to success."

~ Ed Seykota

"You should expect the unexpected in this business; expect the extreme. Don't think in terms of boundaries that limit what the market might do. If there is any lesson I have learned in the nearly twenty years that I've been in this business, it is that the unexpected and the impossible happen every now and then."

~ Richard Dennis

If you don't have effective business systems in place to support your trading, you will find it more difficult to generate a meaningful amount of wealth from the market. You might get a few pips here and there, but without the proper infrastructure you will hit a roadblock when you get to a certain level, or worse, you will suffer a large loss on the profits you have taken so long to accumulate. It pays to be prepared before that happens.

In this chapter, we go into the systems you will need to have in place to trade Forex with confidence and at size, including:

- Risk management
- Trade assessment and execution
- Recording and monitoring your performance
- Trading strategy evaluation
- Contingency planning.

By adding these elements to your trading plan, you are entering the realm of the professional. These are the tools hedge funds use to run their trading business. Indeed, this lesson has been put together with the help of a friend of mine who runs one such fund.

TRADING IS A BUSINESS NOT A HOBBY

"I've always viewed trading as a business."

~ Victor Sperandeo

For the trader who is serious about making money, trading is not an interesting hobby, filled with chart gazing and reading news; it is a business. This means lots of hard work, implementing the trading business systems they need for success—just as if if they were starting a business in any other industry. These systems should be written in a business plan. It does not have to be a stuffy plan. It should be one that is a pleasure to work with, but make sure you write it down.

YOUR FIRST JOB AS A TRADER IS TO MANAGE RISK

"Risk control is the most important thing in trading."

~ Paul Tudor Jones

"You are not a trader; you are a risk manager."

~ Larry Benedict

The first systems you need to build in to your trading business plan are risk-management systems. Through these systems, you protect your trading account from damaging losses from:

- Poor trading

- A fault with your trading system, or

- A fault with your position-sizing model, or

- A run of losses due to market conditions.

Your position-sizing strategy is also an important part of your risk management. Position sizing is the "how much to place on each trade" aspect of trading. Here, we discuss account-wide rules to be implemented along with your position-sizing model.

Maximum Loss in a Day/Week/Month

If you experience a loss on your account that reaches a certain level, you will need to take action to limit further losses. This could be to stop trading altogether, or it could be to reduce your position size. Depending on your trading style, this could be a maximum loss in a day, a week, or a month. For example, as mentioned earlier, Market Wizard Michael Platt allows traders in his fund a 3% maximum loss per year. If they lose 3%, then they have their allocation cut in half. If they then lose a further 3% of the reduced allocation, they are out of a job (harsh but effective).

Maximum Number of Trades at any One Time

The more positions you have on at any one time, the more difficult they become to manage. If your positions are correlated, you can essentially end up with one big position instead of several smaller ones. You will want to decide how many trades you will have on at one time and how many correlated positions you will allow yourself to take. You may want to limit yourself to a maximum of four or five trades at any one time. But this does depend on your approach.

Maximum Leverage on the Account

Even if you have very few trades, if you are scaling in, you could end up exposed to a very large position. One way of protecting yourself from this risk is to limit the maximum amount of leverage you will have on the account. For example, you could set a maximum leverage of 10:1. This maximum leverage could either be set physically on your account by your broker, or you will need to calculate it yourself as you place trades.

ASSESSING TRADES

When you find an opportunity to place a trade, you want to have a system for assessing if it is the right trade for you. This is not meant to be a time consuming investigation but rather a quick check to see whether the trade fits your portfolio, like a hedge fund manager would do with their trading team.

In a hedge fund, the positions and trades are combined to express an overall picture of the fund's view, and they are carefully considered re: weightings and what synthetic cross positions are created by introducing another position. While you don't have to go this far and can treat the trades as individual, non-correlated trade ideas, you generally will want to quickly consider the following factors.

RISK/REWARD

Check if the trade has a risk/reward ratio you desire. Preferably, the risk/reward would be greater than 3:1, but 1:1 or less can be okay for shorter-term trades.

TIMEFRAME

Check if the trade matches your trading horizon. If you are predominately a short-term trader, you might not want to place trades that are long term or vice versa.

CORRELATIONS

"I...designed a lot of risk management systems [and] I paid strict attention to the correlations of all my positions."

~ Bruce Kovner

"Controlling Correlations is the key to managing risk."

~ Michael Platt

Check your current positions for correlations. If the new trade is correlated with your current positions, you may not wish to take it. For example: if you are already short the EUR/USD and you get a recommendation to short the EUR/AUD, you may decide not take it, to avoid holding too big a position short in the EUR.

HEDGING AND SYNTHETIC POSITIONS

If you have current trades, then a trade could act as a hedge to your current positions or effectively create a synthetic position you did not intend to have. For example: if you are long USD/JPY and take a short EUR/JPY position, then, in effect, you have a short EUR/USD position.

POSITION-SIZING MODEL

When you get to place a trade, you will need to decide what position-sizing model you will use on the trade. For example, you may use different position-sizing rules for short-term and long-term trades.

SEPARATE ACCOUNTS FOR SEPARATE STRATEGIES

One of the keys to successful trading is simplicity. Using different trading strategies in one account can be a major source of trading mistakes. Set up separate trading accounts for each strategy. This does not mean separate accounts for each type of entry signal you have, as one strategy can have many. Rather, if you have two completely different sets of rules (such as day trading vs. long-term trading), then operate each of them in a different account.

This will help with the analysis and evaluation of the strategy, as well as help you to stay disciplined, since there will be no hiding of a losing strategy behind a winning one.

USE MULTIPLE BROKERS

It is preferable that you use different brokers for each account, rather than having several accounts with the same broker. This will protect you from counter-party risk, i.e., your broker going bust, which is, unfortunately, all too common.

RECORDING AND MONITORING TRADES

When asked if they record their trades, the majority of amateur traders say no. When a professional is asked if they record their trades, the answer is invariably yes. Spot the difference?

If you don't record your trades, it's hard to know what you are doing right or wrong, so it's hard to make meaningful changes to your trading strategy. Luckily, recording trades can be partially automated by services such as Tradervue. Tradervue is preferred, as it allows you to record R-multiples and will calculate the quality of the system using Van Tharp's System Quality Number (SQN) method. It also has journaling functions.

It's critical you don't neglect this part of your business planning, as over the long term, it will generate success for you.

Imagine this:

- You place 20 trades, and record your results.
- You work out what worked and what didn't, and make changes to your plan.
- Place another 20 trades.
- Rinse and repeat.
- By following this process of eliminating mistakes and testing, you eventually get your trading to a point where it is profitable.

TRADING STRATEGY EVALUATION

"We test our criteria to make sure they are timeless and universal."

~ Ray Dalio

Trading strategy evaluation is a critical facet of managing your trading like a business. Not only does it help you improve, it guides your position sizing. The better the trading system you have, the more you can risk on each trade. When you are evaluating your system, you want to:

- Check that you have clear objectives and a matching position-sizing algorithm

- Check that the strategy meets the objectives of the trading system plan

- Be able to understand:
  - Each part of the strategy
  - Why it works
  - Its edges
  - Under what conditions it works and does not work

- Understand what the underlying beliefs of the strategy are

- How the strategy performs in the six primary market types

- Make sure the strategy includes robust rules and processes

- What psychological issues are arising when trading the system?

This process of evaluation should be done on a regular basis. It is also good to check the SQN of your system over a rolling, 30-day basis, in order to spot any degradation in the performance of your system before it's too late.

AVOIDING SYSTEM DEATH

"The strategy is always changing. It is a research war."

~ Michael Platt

"Strategies that have been based on the manager's most recent experience will work until they invariably don't work."

~Ray Dalio

System death. Nothing is forever, and I'm sorry to say that includes any system(s) you may use. What worked yesterday might not work tomorrow, and what worked a year ago might never work again. Perhaps the market type changed, or your edge simply evaporated. Fear not; with enough confidence and preparation, you can quite easily protect your account in case of system failure. Preparing for a disaster will also give you the confidence to manage and hopefully even avoid any potential disaster.

KNOW YOUR MARKET TYPE

Every good system is built—and maintained—to be compatible with certain market types and may be incompatible with others. To avoid this pitfall, don't be shy to stop trading—or to switch systems—for a while until conditions are favorable again.

A FEW COMMON REASONS FOR STRATEGIES FAILING:

Poorly designed systems. A system might be successfully back-tested on past market data, but this is no guarantee of success when trading live, as anything can happen.

Conditions change. Your edge came and went—maybe it became a more popular strategy and stopped working, or perhaps it relied on something that's simply no longer true.

Trading errors. The system works, but the trader can't make the most of it for one reason or another (for example, due to subpar risk management or position-sizing errors).

Don't Hold on When You Should Let Go

When you find a working system and trade with it, it's a matter of when—not if—it stops working. All systems eventually need to be buried, rotated, tweaked, or rebuilt from the ground up. The eventual decline and demise of your strategy is nobody's fault—that is, unless you keep using it after it starts demonstrably losing.

Have more than one system. This will allow you to trade confidently in more than one market type, as well as giving you immediate options for replacement systems when necessary.

Play it safe. Protect your account first and foremost. If you think a system is on its last legs, take this into account in your position sizing. Leave less hanging over the edge in times of danger.

Divest yourself emotionally. If your system's results are dwindling, it's not a direct reflection of your abilities. Holding on to a dying system simply because you developed it will cost you a lot more than it needs to, and probably sooner rather than later.

Keep a close eye on your results, and make sure to compare them from day to day, week to week, or month to month. This is the best way to see intuitively whether your system is failing. From there, you can adjust it if necessary, or do away with it altogether.

On a Scale of "Poor" to "Excellent"...

Managing to avoid a catastrophic system failure is actually quite simple; it just takes preparation, confidence, and honest evaluation. If you know what your system should be returning and what it is returning, you can perform a simple expectancy vs. results evaluation as follows:

Example: you place 30 trades, each with a $100 stop-loss and a $200 take-profit order. It's your lucky day, and every single trade brings in the target. So your result is two times your risk; you could say the expectancy for now is 2.

If you had manually taken between $120 and $150 profit in each position, then your expectancy would be between 1.2 and 1.5, which would be a great result.

If 20/30 trades had lost $100, and 10/30 had made $200, that's $2,000 vs. $2,000, and so your expectancy would be zero or breakeven for that period.

The idea is to track your system's expectancy over the last 30 trades (i.e., rolling), and stop using it altogether around the point where you can only really expect to break even.

Excellent	Expectancy above 1.5
Very Good	Expectancy between 0.6 – 1.5
Good	Expectancy between 0.2 – 0.5
Breakeven	Expectancy between -0.1 – 0.1
Poor	Expectancy below -0.1

Eventually, if your system starts to degrade over time because you're keeping a rolling, 30-trade evaluation, you will see the proof. If this happens, your options include:

- Trading smaller positions.

- Assigning less money to that system (and perhaps more to another subsequently).

- Decide not to use the system at all anymore. You might try to fix it, or simply move on.

Make It Your Own

Every trader is different, from preferences and methods to expectations and worldview. One trader's good is another trader's excellent, and vice versa.

If you're happy with 0.4, then a drop from 1.1 to 0.4 doesn't have to be perceived as a disaster, in and of itself. You don't have to abandon ship right when the number dips drastically; you simply have the framework in place to deploy the life raft when the time does come.

The real objective here is to prevent a system from causing damage in its last throes, and so expectancy starts to mean more in this context as it approaches 0, because going past -0.1 willingly is the definition of trading a losing system.

Sometimes, a perceived degradation will be due to temporary noise in the market, sometimes, it will be an unfortunate news spike or three, and sometimes, it will be because your system is genuinely doomed.

The key is to evaluate properly, and learn to recognize the difference, so you can step in with the discipline and confidence we were discussing earlier.

Another Way to Monitor Your System's Performance

Some traders prefer to allocate capital across two or more of their systems based on the systems' respective equity curves. If system A's curve is performing well, you might want to give it 65% of your capital, and size your positions accordingly.

If system B's curve is firmly on the way down, you might be happy only to give it the remaining 35% or less. You would then keep checking on the curve and adjusting as necessary. At a certain point, you might decide to toss that strategy away.

Using either this method or the evaluation method above, you will have all the feedback you need to avoid a strategic meltdown in the long run.

This is arguably a more reactive method, but some traders simply find it more intuitive. Once again, this is going to come down to preference.

CONTINGENCY PLANNING

"My mental rehearsal for a catastrophic event is to picture a doctor in a triage situation. He's in a battlefield emergency operating room. In come 50 bodies. Some are going to live; some are going to die. The doctor has been trained to handle the situation. He's going to make all the necessary decisions... he is calm and collected, not nervous."

~ Tom Basso

When you are trading small sizes, contingency planning is not so important. But the more you develop your trading and the larger sizes you trade, the more relevant it becomes. There are many horror stories of traders who have had an unexpected event interrupt their trading and wipe out years' worth of profits. Even if not that dramatic, unexpected events can cause a large loss in the blink of an eye.

The contingency planning of major hedge funds is as in-depth as the strategic planning in a modern military organization. That is, it is extremely thorough. Market Wizard Tom Basso plans how to run his entire hedge fund off a laptop and mobile phone for example. He then conducts "dry runs", where he tests out his systems in the case of a disaster affecting his business.

There is a story about Basso, that when a fellow trader called him, he hung up the phone, saying he was busy and needed to keep the line free, as a hurricane had hit. The trader had not heard about a hurricane, and when he checked the weather, it turned out the conditions were perfectly clear. Apparently, Basso was conducting a dry run of his contingency plans! Here is a list of contingencies you will need to plan for if you want to trade at a reasonable size. Some responses to the situation are also listed, though you will need to make them your own.

188

THINGS THAT IMPACT TRADERS PERSONALLY

Sickness or death of a family member or close friend: Stop trading for twenty-four hours. Assess whether trading should resume or be put on hold.

Emergency with the family comes up when trading: Close all positions. Assess whether trading should resume or be put on hold.

THINGS THAT AFFECT YOUR ENVIRONMENT

There is noise in your environment that affects you: Put on a headset or ear muffs. If it is consistent, then consider moving to another environment.

EVENTS RELATED TO YOUR BROKER

Your broker accidentally gets your account balance wrong: Contact the broker and inform them. Work with them until the correct balance is restored.

Your broker has an outage: Check social media for information. Contact the broker by phone, chat, or social media, if required.

Your broker has an outage that lasts for greater than twenty-four hours: Move trading to a backup broker. Contact the broker, and conduct a review.

Your broker has an outage during a major news event or with a position that does not have a stop-loss: Place a hedging position with another broker. Contact the broker by phone, chat, or on social media.

PROBLEMS OR DISASTERS WITH EQUIPMENT

The charting platform goes down: Switch to a different platform (traders should have a number of platforms on their computer).

The computer goes down: Switch to back-up computer or mobile platform. Contact another trader or friend, and use their computer.

Laws and Regulatory Disasters, which Are Good for the Government but Bad for the Trading Strategy.

Margin requirements are changed: Assess impact on trading system. Consider moving to a different regulatory environment or adjusting the trading system. If required, reduce position sizing in the meantime.

Market Disasters

Unscheduled major news occurs when in a position: Assess whether the news has a 20% or greater chance to cause a loss of more than 1R. If so, then close the position. Otherwise, monitor closely.

Trading System Disasters

The system performs outside of expectations: Reduce position size to 10% of original size. Shift trading to a back-up system.

Psychological Problems

You trade with below 90% efficiency: Stop trading for twenty-four hours. Talk to a fellow trader to discuss and assess next steps.

You become unhappy: Stop trading for twenty-four hours. Talk to a fellow trader to discuss and assess next steps.

Environment Disasters

Earthquake, flood, hurricane, or other disaster that affects the environment that the trader is operating in: Stop trading for twenty-four hours after the event occurs. Assess potential for power to return and if it is safe to remain in the environment. If it is not safe to remain in the environment, then move with equipment and family to a safe location. Once safe, if there is Internet access, then steps can be taken to continue trading.

GET SERIOUS AND START PLANNING

Take a look at your conduct in the market, and decide if you are treating trading like a hobby or a business.

(Hint: If you are doing the things in this lesson, then you are treating trading like a business; if you are not, then you are likely treating it like a hobby.)

If you are not giving trading the gravitas that it deserves, then stop and assess what you need to change. Start by writing down your risk-management rules and sticking to them. As time goes on, revisit this lesson, and start working on your monitoring and recording systems before moving on to contingency planning.

If you do these things, you are creating the systems that will form the lifeblood of your trading, and you will be able to support the growth of your trading account to a large size—without any big hiccups along the way.

THE MASTER TRADER MINDSET

"There are three primary factors involved in duplicated success—Beliefs, mental states, and mental strategies."

~ Van Tharp

By immersing yourself in the mentality of some of history's greatest traders, the understanding of what it takes to be successful becomes more integrated in your trading. Here are six common themes amongst how the market wizards think. All of them:

- Credit their success to discipline
- Take a rational and practical approach to money management
- Have no boundaries and are open to everything
- Think against the herd
- Play the good hands, and drop out of the poor hands
- Trade bigger when they are trading better.

If you adopt these mindsets as your own, I can guarantee you will become a much better trader.

THE EXCEPTION THAT PROVES THE RULE

One of the more interesting things about the Market Wizards is that one might hold the exact opposite view from another, yet both are highly successful in their own right. Aside from this, speaking to the fact that it's important for a trader to have a method that suits them, it means it's possible to find contradicting evidence for many of the mindsets in this chapter.

One obvious example is the concept of cutting your losses short and letting profits run. There are examples of traders who either let their losses run or cut their profits short and make spectacular profits doing so. This does not mean the overall mindset is wrong, just that there are many ways to be successful, depending on your market model.

What I attempt to do in this chapter is create a "glide path". I look for the commonalities between top traders, and focus on the things that we, as retail traders, can apply in our approach to the markets. I will outline the contrary view where I can. Let's get started with one of the most commonly known but least well-understood master trader mindsets—discipline.

THE MOST IMPORTANT THING IS DISCIPLINE

Imagine a trader with no discipline. They fail to follow their rules. They enter and exit on a whim, or, perhaps, much worse, they fail to have any trading rules at all. Contrast this with a highly disciplined trader, who executes their plan flawlessly (at size) without exception, even when it seems like the most difficult thing to do. Which one would you rather be? The answer is obvious but perhaps somewhat elusive to achieve. So how to be disciplined?

There are a number of mindsets highly disciplined traders share.

TRADING IS A GAME

"I like the game. I think it's a great challenge. It's also an easy game to keep score of."

~ Bill Lipschitz

Many of the traders interviewed in the *Market Wizards* books viewed trading as a game. If you view trading as a game, then making a mistake is necessarily a failure to follow your rules. Viewed through this lens, perfect play becomes a lot easier to work toward.

Whether you make or lose money on any individual trade is *not* important. What is important is that you follow the rules of the game.

MONEY IS NOT IMPORTANT

"In our business you have to have a total disregard for money. You can't trade for money."

~ Tom Baldwin

Top traders view money as unimportant. Of course, they want to make money, and they are very respectful of their capital and profits, but it's not *about the money*. It's about following the correct trading processes. If they do that, then the money will come. Instead, if your focus is on the money you are making or losing, you tend to make emotional decisions based on fear and greed. Focus your total attention on trading well, and let the results take care of themselves.

DON'T CARE IF YOU WIN OR LOSE ON A TRADE

"I usually don't get excited by winners; I'm too busy looking for the next trade."

~ Steve Watson

Not every trade you place is going to be a winner. Some will win, and some will lose. It's important as a trader not to get invested in the results of any one trade. When you trade, control your emotions. Strive for a sense of balance, no matter what the market does. If you have a win, don't get elated. If you have a loss, don't get upset about it. Instead, be happy simply that you have followed your rules no matter the outcome.

TRADING IS LIKE ROLLING A DICE LOADED IN YOUR FAVOR

When you place a trade, it's helpful to think that it's like rolling dice loaded in your favor. Trading is a game of probabilities, where the results of any one trade does not matter. Over time, if you "continue to roll the dice", your losses will be far outweighed by the profits from the wins generated by your system's edge (your "loaded dice").

This means that as a trader, your job is to follow your system, irrespective of whether the last trade was a win or a loss. If your system does something that results in losses, that's just part of the system, and so it's nothing to be greatly worried about.

THINK OF THE NEXT TRADE AS THE FIRST IN THE NEXT 1000 YOU ARE GOING TO DO

As humans, we tend to over value recent results, so it is helpful to put the trade in the context of your trading lifespan. The reality is the trade is one of potentially thousands you will place over your career as a trader. While it might be nice for the trade to go for you, the market is going to do what it does, irrespective of your feelings. If you can put the trade in this perspective, it becomes much easier to calmly accept the results—good or bad.

A PLAN FORCES DISCIPLINE

"Planning to get out before putting on the trade is a means of enforcing emotional discipline."

~ Victor Sperandeo

Without a written plan, it is incredibly difficult to be disciplined. If you trade with no plan, you are what is termed a "non-rules-based" discretionary trader. That is, a trader who enters positions on feelings, tips, or simply what looks good at the time. By having a set of written rules, processes, and objectives that you follow when you trade, you are exercising discipline. You enter the realm of "rules-based" discretionary traders, where Market Wizard Van Tharp suggests that 90% of successful traders live (the other 10% are mechanical traders).

HAVE A CORE PHILOSOPHY: WITHOUT A CORE PHILOSOPHY YOU ARE NOT GOING TO BE ABLE TO HOLD ON TO YOUR POSITION

"You must fully understand, strongly believe in, and be totally committed to your trading philosophy."

~ Richard Driehaus

As well as having a plan, it is very useful to develop a core trading philosophy. By knowing what you are trying to achieve and by being very comfortable about your trading, you can continue about your trading business with a minimum of fuss or emotion.

It's by really, truly knowing what you are about as a trader that your trading discipline goes to another level. This is why it is difficult to trade someone else's plan.

You can have a great set of rules, but if you are not in tune with the reasons behind the rules, then you will find them tricky or even impossible to follow mistake free. This is particularly true when it comes to trading at larger sizes or holding on to a winning position. Without understanding your system's edge and why you are holding on to the position, you will be tempted to grab your profit prematurely.

OBJECTIVELY EVALUATE YOUR PROGRESS

If you are holding yourself accountable for following your plan, you will instill a large degree of discipline in your performance. By being honest with yourself when evaluating your progress, you will pick up on the things that are hampering you or areas where you are making mistakes.

A good way to do this is to establish a review process for your trading. This could be done daily, weekly, or on each individual trade. This is one task that comes highly recommended if you want to achieve peak trading performance. Furthermore, it will force you to accept unpleasant truths about your trading.

Perhaps you think you have been disciplined when you have not been. There is a story in the *Market Wizards* books about an amateur trader who believes his wife is hiding his trading statements, when in fact, he is subconsciously hiding them himself to avoid facing his losses. While this is an extreme example, sometimes we are doing things we don't realize we are doing until we take the time to review it.

HAVE A RATIONAL AND PRACTICAL APPROACH TO RISK MANAGEMENT

"Ironically, even though money management is more important than the price model, mathematically, it's the more tractable problem"

~ William Eckhart

RISK MANAGEMENT

We all hate buzzwords, but it's hard to get away from them. Initially, when we hear the term "risk management", we are intrigued. After a while, we realize everyone is using the damn words, and they lose their meaning. But if you want to trade successfully, risk management is not something you should dismiss.

All the market wizards heavily emphasize risk management as being crucial to their longevity. It is ingrained in their trading mindset. Thankfully, risk management is not rocket science (though some market wizards are quite complex in how they implement it). Rather, it is a matter of being practical and taking a logical approach. It's generally about keeping track of what you are doing and applying common sense.

This starts with the old trading adage of cutting your losses short and letting your profits run.

CUTTING LOSSES SHORT AND LETTING PROFITS RUN

"Two of the cardinal sins of trading—giving losses too much rope and taking profits prematurely—are both attempts to make the current position more likely to succeed, to the severe detriment of long-term performance."

~ William Eckhart

A trade that works 50% of the time can be very profitable if you apply a good money-management plan that keeps your losses smaller than your wins. While it is not universal amongst the market wizards, some of whom practice high-probability trading (a high percentage of small, winning trades), a lot of them attribute a large part of their success to holding on to their winning trades and quickly getting rid of losing ones.

PLAY GREAT DEFENSE FIRST

"To commit very little capital, take on very little risk, and still make a significant return consistently—They are a very smart firm."

~ Alphonse Fletcher Jr., discussing Bear Sterns philosophy

A powerful risk-management mindset is to manage the downside and not to worry about the upside. If you have a good system, the upside will come if you preserve your capital. Good traders have very little tolerance for losses.

If you lose your core capital, you are out of the game. It's as simple as that. This is particularly true for retail traders. The longer you are around, the greater chance you have of learning what you need to do to start making money.

It's also important to protect your profits...not just your principal capital. Don't be cavalier when you are in profit. Just because you are playing with the market's money does not mean you should be any less respectful of it.

Finally, if you think you are wrong, or that the market is moving against you, and you don't know why, take in half. Don't hold on and hope; be proactive in taking action to protect your capital. Remember, defense first.

TRADE SIZE IS MORE IMPORTANT THAN THE ENTRY POINT

"Varying the position size can be as important as the entry methodology."

~ Edward Thorp

A common theme amongst market wizards is that "how much you trade" is more important than the entry price. Your position size—not your entry—will determine your profit or loss on the trade. Controlling the size of your loss is the key to risk management, so this area should receive a lot of your attention.

The trade size impacts not only the profit or loss on the position but also liquidity. You need to manage the liquidity on the trade, so you can get out quickly when you are wrong. If you get stuck in a large position that you cannot easily exit, you could be faced with a risk-management disaster.

Risk management becomes more complicated when you are managing multiple positions. Don't concentrate too much of your capital on any one trade or group of trades, and make sure you always know exactly where you stand on an account level.

You can be right and still end up losing if you use too much leverage. If your highly leveraged position experiences an adverse move, you might not be able to bear it, and your broker could close out your trade at an inopportune moment—even if it would have eventually gone for you in the end. If you wake up thinking a position is too big, cut down on your trade size.

KNOW YOUR RISK/REWARD POTENTIAL

Knowing the potential risk/reward on the trade is a critical part of risk management. You should only take trades where you can generate a decent risk/reward ratio.

Generally, you will want to structure your trades to be right skewed—that is, the maximum loss is limited, but the potential upside is unlimited. In addition, it's important to understand the risk/reward of the trade as it stands dynamically (not just when you put it on).

BE PREPARED TO DEAL WITH SITUATIONS THAT MIGHT SEEM STATISTICALLY IMPOSSIBLE

Always expect the unexpected from the markets. Statistically improbable events occur far more often than they theoretically should. Work out what you will do when you experience one of these events in your risk-management plan.

Just ask the founders of Long Term Capital Management about how they brought the financial markets to the brink of disaster in the late 1990s by assuming that the "statistically impossible" would not happen. Or ask anybody who experienced the 1987 Black Monday crash, or any of the several flash crashes that should "never" have happened in a rational market. If you are not prepared and stick around when the market is severely against you, eventually, they are going to carry you out on a stretcher.

HAVE NO BOUNDARIES, BE OPEN TO EVERYTHING

The market wizards are remarkably open-minded. Though they may hold a strong view in a particular move, if they see evidence to the contrary, they will turn on a dime. They are also uniquely adept at identifying opportunities based on what they see in front of them. Stuart Walton sums up the attitude colorfully when he states:

"My philosophy is to float like a jelly fish, and let the market push me where it wants to go."

This flexible mindset is essential both in avoiding losses and in uncovering opportunities.

BEING WRONG IS ACCEPTABLE, BUT STAYING WRONG IS TOTALLY UNACCEPTABLE.

"The main thing is that every trader has to be honest about his or her weakness and deal with it. If you can't learn to do that you will not survive as a trader."

~ Mark Cook

Good traders have humility. They have the ability to admit when things are not going their way and make a new decision. They know that part of trading is being wrong. Sometimes, well-constructed ideas just don't play out as hoped. This is okay; it's a natural part of trading. But what is destructive to your trading account is being wrong and stubborn. If your ego gets in the way of admitting that the market is not doing what you anticipated and causes you to ignore the signs you need to make a change, then that is unacceptable.

GOOD TRADING IS NOT ABOUT BEING RIGHT. IT'S ABOUT MAKING MONEY.

In fact, for many people, the need to be right gets in the way of making money. In trading, it's not about being right; it's about how much money you make when you are right.

Stephen Cohen suggests that his top trader makes money only 63% of the time, and most traders only get 50-55% of their ideas correct, even though in the end they come out way in front. To make money, you have to be prepared to change your opinion. You should hold no loyalty to your positions. Anything that has happened up to the present time is history, and if things change, you need to change with them, too. Clinging to wrong beliefs is a recipe for sub-optimal returns. If you are wrong, get out, and focus on something that is looking more promising.

THE MIND IS LIKE A PARACHUTE—IT'S ONLY GOOD WHEN IT'S OPEN

"I sit back and try to see what idea rises to the top."

~ Stuart Walton

Don't be picky about how you make your money. Keep an open mind to the opportunities the market is presenting you. This is about being conscious. Consciousness is one of the trader's most critical tools—be self-aware and open to ideas that are presented to you.

Keep your trading models as flexible as possible, so you give yourself the ability to jump on the opportunities when they come your way. Have a curious mind, and continually ask why—why do you have that view, what is the evidence, and what can you do to best capitalize on it?

BE YOUR OWN PERSON AND THINK AGAINST THE HERD

"It's not enough to simply have the insight to see something apart from the rest of the crowd, you also need to have the courage to act on it. It's very difficult to be different from the rest of the crowd the majority of the time, which by definition is what you are doing if you're a successful trader."

~ Bill Lipschitz

A critical ingredient of a master-trader mindset is a maverick mind. The market wizards have the courage to act against conventional wisdom. If you can do the opposite of what the people around you are going to do, you should be able to make a good return. The market wizards tend to have a large dose of contrarian thinking. They are quite comfortable acting against the herd. They tend to hold little regard for the opinions of Wall Street analysts and are relaxed in taking a contrary view.

TO WIN, YOU NEED TO ACT LIKE THE MINORITY, BUT TIMING IS IMPORTANT

"In order to win as a contrarian, you need to get the timing right."

~ Michael Steinhardt

When no one wants to do it, sometimes, there is a great opportunity, but being a contrarian also has a large degree of risk. If you are trading against consensus, you need to be very careful about the timing.

For example, Michael Steinhardt took a huge position short US bonds when the interest rates were near 17%, and experts were calling them to go to 30%. Many others who thought bonds were too high at lower levels were wiped out, but this turned out to be Steinhardt's best trade up to that point in time. He credits his success to getting his timing right, but even he came close to being wiped out.

To get the timing right, many of the market wizards look to find catalysts that trigger the move down. This could be a news event, or it could be price, acting contrary to expectations when news is announced.

IT'S A BIG MISTAKE TO SURRENDER THE DECISION-MAKING RESPONSIBILITY TO SOMEONE ELSE

"You have to follow your own light."

~Michael Marcus

A number of the market wizards had large losses when they first began trading. Generally, this was due to poor discipline and risk management. For some, it was also a result of not trusting their judgment or from following tips from brokers or friends. If you surrender the decision-making process to others, it becomes difficult to follow through on the trade. Should you close it out, or hold on? Because it's not your decision to enter, you will find it difficult to know when to exit.

Jack Schwager, the author of the *Market Wizards* books, relates a story where he followed a tip from an accomplished Elliot wave trader and continued to break all his rules as the trade went against him. He continued to hold it, losing money and not knowing when to get out. Along with this, never let your market decisions be restricted or influenced by what others think when you are in the trade.

When Mark Minervini first began trading, he held on to a large losing trade because he did not want to get teased by his broker for picking a losing stock. Needless to say, that experience did not end well for him. Be your own man or woman, and have the courage to walk your own path.

PLAY THE GOOD HANDS AND DROP OUT OF THE POOR HANDS

"By trading less, I was picking my best spots."

~ Mark Cook

Top traders know when to go for the kill. If they have a great deal of conviction about a trade, they have the courage and discipline to trade a much larger size. Similarly, if they don't know what's going on, they simply just don't play.

Their trades are very calculated, and they have very good reasons for putting them on. They only enter the market when their edge is clear, and they are quick to drop out of those trades that don't give them the best opportunities for a large return.

The elite traders combine risk management and discipline with the patience to wait for high-conviction ideas, and then the courage to act on them by taking a large position and holding on until either they are proven wrong, or they have reached their maximum profit potential. This is perhaps the crux of what it means to be a market wizard. If you can adopt this mentality and have half-decent ideas, then you are going to be a very successful trader.

Wait Until There Is Money Lying Around the Corner and Then Go and Pick It Up

"I just don't play."

~ Jim Rogers

The first ingredient of this mentality is patience. Top traders will wait until the stars align before getting into a trade. Your top 10 ideas will perform better than your top 100, so if you have the patience to wait for the very good ones, it will reflect in your performance. There is no need to rush, as the opportunity will come. You can't control when acceptable opportunities appear, but you can conserve your capital until those opportunities appear.

Trade Bigger When You Have Conviction on a Trade

"The speculator can choose to only bet when the odds are in his favor. That is an important positional advantage."

~ Larry Hite

When you do see an opportunity, go at full force, or don't go at all—don't just dabble. Be confident in varying your position size to trade much bigger when you have conviction. This does not mean you should not be placing trades in the meantime. A lot of good positions eventuate over time from a small start. If you have a good idea, you can take an initial position, and see how it plays out. By placing a trade on your idea like this, it focuses your attention. Many of the market wizards practice this type of scale-in approach.

But don't place trades for the sake of it. Operate with real intent to go for your good ideas, and be aggressive in making the most out of them. When you get it right, you want to get it right in a big way. Trade smaller for lower-conviction trades and larger for higher-conviction ones. If you are uncertain, then tread very lightly with your risk capital, and err on the side of caution if you lack conviction on the trade.

Don't Confuse Activity with Accomplishment

"I don't do anything until all the pieces fit."

~ James Rogers

Many traders spend a lot of time trading, but only a small amount of their trades generate the majority of their profits. It's the old 80/20 rule. 20% of their activity generates 80% of their profits.

See if you can isolate the things that really work for you. Work out which types of trades are the ones that make you the most profit, and focus on those. Less is often more when it comes to trading. It takes discipline and self-awareness to stop doing what is not working, but you can dramatically improve your trading by focusing on what works best for you and putting the rest aside.

Pick an Area and Become an Expert

To develop high-conviction ideas, you don't want to spread yourself too thin. If you can become an expert in a particular area or technique, it can provide you with a significant advantage over others who are trading with a lesser degree of expertise.

It can be good to remember that a number of the market wizards have the same degree of access to information that you have, making it very much possible to become an expert in a chosen field. This will allow you to really focus on the trades with the best potential, and drop out of the ones that are less likely.

DON'T PARTICIPATE IN TOO MANY MARKETS AT ANY ONE TIME

Once you are in your high-conviction positions, you need to be very focused on them. If you look to diversify into too many positions, your best trades might not get the attention they need.

Give yourself a limit of a number of trades you will have on at any one time. This might mean you miss out on some opportunities, but that is okay. Your job is not to be on every trade but to make as much as you can from your best ones. In saying that, you should still be looking for the best potential performance at the current time. If a better trade comes along, be comfortable rotating out of your current trade into the new one.

THE BETTER YOU'RE DOING, THE BIGGER YOU CAN PLAY

Some traders are able to turn small amounts of money into very large amounts. It might be tempting to believe that this is because of risky trading practices, and sometimes, it can be. If you take large positions compared to your account size, you could get lucky. If you are willing to take big risks, you can earn big rewards.

Of course, while this may work for a while, it's not a recipe for long-term success.

As Market Wizard Ed Seykota says, success in trading is about longevity, and taking big risks in your trading account is not the way to stay in the game for the long run.

The thing that separates the top traders from the traders that do not make it is that they learn to temper their risk taking with risk management. They have developed processes for risk taking that protects their capital, while really letting them profit when things are going well.

You Can Be Far More Aggressive When You Are Making Profits

To make large profits, you can increase your bet sizes after periods of high profitability. This allows you to take large position sizes while avoiding risk to your core capital. This is the "market's money" concept. Market's money is where you risk your profits—on a trade or on your account—to trade at a larger size.

To do this, once you're comfortably in profit, you simply increase your position size on a high-confidence trade. This process means you can only get hit when you are being paid but not from a standing start, and you give yourself the best chance to be successful when you are risking more. If you get too careful about risking your gains, you're not going to be able to extract a large profit.

When You Are Feeling More Attuned, Gradually Increase Your Position Size

When you are doing things correctly, you can expand your involvement in the market. This is a very common mentality amongst the top currency traders, along with the flipside of trading smaller when things are not going well. If you are picking it well and the market is going in your favor, be prepared to gradually increase your trade size. This will mean you make the most out of the good times when you are most attuned.

It Takes Courage to Be a Pig

"The way to build long-term returns is through preservation of capital and home runs."

~ Stanley Druckenmiller

Stanley Druckenmiller, the heir apparent to George Soros's Quantum Fund, colorfully suggests that for truly superior returns you need to have the "courage to be a pig". In one of his particularly insightful interviews, he says the way to make truly superior profits is to grind it out until you are up 30-40%, and then, if you have the conviction, go for a 100% year.

You work hard with well-contained risk, until you have achieved a moderate return. Then you really go for it, and increase the position size on your best ideas. Again, this method allows you to keep your risk to your core capital small, while still having the potential for very large returns.

INCREASING YOUR POSITION SIZE ON A WINNING STREAK CAN LEAD TO LARGE LOSS

"I've always had my biggest setbacks after my biggest victories. I was careless."

~ Marty Schwartz

This is the downside to increasing your position size when you have profits. If you are on a winning streak and you increase your position size, you are guaranteed to have your biggest loss. Other good traders, particularly those involved in system trading, prefer to keep their risk small and constant. This is the exception that proves the rule. It depends on the personality of the trader or the requirements of the system.

INTEGRATING THE MASTER-TRADER MINDSET

There is no denying the importance of your mindset when it comes to trading. To integrate your newly adopted mindset, you can follow this three-step process. Firstly, write down your mindset, and keep it by your trading desk. When you are making trading decisions, refer to what you have written.

Notice when you make mistakes, and conduct self-work so you stop making them. If you do this, your trading performance should go up several notches. Trust me, you'll notice the difference.

How to Make Foundational Change to Your Trading Psychology

"The emotional burden of trading is substantial."

~ Bruce Kovner

"The best traders have no ego."

~ Tom Baldwin

Mastery requires a willingness to commit to changing yourself. It's through self-work that you get from where you are to where you want to be.

When we approach the markets, we bring with us our personal problems and a number of biases that arise from the way our brain works (thanks evolution!) In many ways we are poorly wired to be good traders. Our natural inclination is to cut our profits short and to hold on to losses—the exact opposite of what works.

Over time, if we can work through our issues, not only will we become much better traders, it can have great benefit to our lives. Many traders report that the self-development they have gone through to become a good trader has had a transformation impact on their personal life, too.

Trading Is 100% Psychology

"Psychology motivates the quality of analysis and puts it to use. Psychology is the driver, and analysis is the roadmap."

~ Ed Seykota

Market Wizard Van Tharp believes that trading is 100% psychology. When you are trading the market, you are trading not the market itself but your beliefs about the market. Your beliefs are 100% psychological, thus trading is, too. Tharp believes anyone can be taught to trade by modeling the mental states and strategies of top traders. If you know what they do, and you can copy them, then you will be successful.

When he says this, he is not referring to the trading strategy a trader might use; rather he is talking about the way they conduct themselves in the market. This includes emotional control, discipline, viewing trading as a game, not caring about money, etc. I have covered many of these skills in this book.

However, even if people understand what it takes to win in the markets, they have "stuff" that comes up that stops them being successful. This "stuff" could be a fear of success, an aversion to risk taking, or a need for excitement, or any number of psychological impediments. Though you know what to do, you fail to execute, and this is where people fall down.

Where does this "stuff" come from? According to Van, from the mess of conflicting parts inside each of us.

YOU ARE A MESS OF CONFLICTING PARTS INSIDE

"If trading is your life, it is a torturous kind of excitement. But if you are keeping your life in balance, then it is fun. All the successful traders I've seen that lasted in this business sooner or later got to that point. They have a balanced life; they have fun outside of trading"

~ *Michael Marcus*

"I was able to separate my ego needs from making money."

~ *Marty Schwartz*

Van's supposition is that each of us has a mess of conflicting parts inside. Each of us might have a trader part, an excitement part, a child part, and a parental part (or 200 or more parts). These parts evolve out of experiences we have had in our life, and they generally have good intentions for us—but not always the best intention for trading.

For example, the excitement part wants to make sure we live life to the fullest, but this is very dangerous when it comes to trading. Trading out of excitement can lead to excessive risk taking and overtrading. You may have a part that was brought up believing rich people are bad, or that money is the root of all evil. This part could hinder your attempts to make money in the market, to help you avoid becoming "bad". As you can see, these parts unwittingly engage in self-sabotage.

I would like to pause now and let you read a two-part article that was published in the Van Tharp Newsletter entitled The Transformative Journey of a Super Trader. This offers a real life example of the power of self-work in your trading and your life.

START WITH THE FOUNDATIONS, AND THE REST WILL CHANGE

"If instead of saying, 'I'm going to do this trade,' you say, 'I'm going to watch myself do this trade', all of a sudden you find the process a lot easier."

~ *Tom Basso*

If you want to transform, surface-level changes will have little lasting impact. If you focus on working on your trading system, you can spend years and get nowhere if the beliefs you are operating from are ill served. Instead, if you change the foundations, all the other elements to your trading will seamlessly click into place. But how to change our foundations? It starts with becoming more aware of one of your parts—the "part" that is your true self or, as Van terms it, your "Divine".

Each of the multitudes of parts inside you masks your true being. In a sense, they are a construct of your ego's desire for control. These parts are the chatter you hear in your mind; your true self is the quiet behind the voices. For those of you who have practiced meditation, you will know what I mean. For others, this may sound alien and probably like nonsense. To that second group, all I would say is to notice what you reject because often that is what you need most.

Once you strip away the chitter-chatter and get to the state of "quiet", you are in a very good place for trading. Free from constraints, you can see the market for what it is, and trade out of the now—not out of fear (which is rooted in thoughts about the past or future).

ZEN AND THE ART OF TRADING

"Every market has a rhythm, and our job as traders is to get in sync with that rhythm. I'm not really trading when I'm doing those trades. There's trading being done, but I'm not doing it."

~ Anonymous

In *The New Market Wizards*, Jack Schwager interviews an unknown trader in the chapter *"Zen and the Art of Trading."*

After conducting the interview, the trader decided he did not want his name published, as he talked about subjects such as eastern mythology, dreams, and intuition and was worried about what his investors might think. In the brief version of the interview that was included, the trader talked about trading without ego.

"There is buying and selling going through me. It's like my personality and ego are not there... It's just an awareness of what will happen. The trick is to differentiate between what you want to happen, and what you know will happen. The intuition knows what will happen."

In *Trading Beyond the Matrix*, Van talks about a super trader of his who trades in a similar state of consciousness. This trader is consistently able to pull large R-multiples from the market in an hour of trading a day.

To achieve deep transformation, focus on exercises that strip away the ego and quiet the chatter of the mind. Anxiety, anger, and other negative emotions begin to disappear, and you become more mindful of what's going on. This serves to make you much better at trading.

Eventually, like the traders in *"Zen and the Art of Trading"* and *Trading Beyond the Matrix*, you learn to form a connection with your Divine (or intuition—call it what works for you) and receive guidance from it (Her/Him/Yourself) in your trading.

CREATING A SELF-DEVELOPMENT PLAN

"The best thing an investor can do, when things go wrong, is to determine how he or she produced those results... the trader that does not own his problems...can continue to repeat his problems because he never gets at the source."

~ Van Tharp

It's beyond the scope of this book to cover the large range of psychological topics that may help you trade better (and there are far more qualified people in the field than me!), but I do want to encourage you to create your own self-development plan.

A self-development plan will aid you in trading without interference from negative emotions or non-useful (for trading) parts. Exactly how you structure your plan will depend on your personality, but it's a good idea to think about what you need to do to have the right mental strategies to trade effectively.

#1 CONDUCT A REVIEW TO IDENTIFY PROBLEM AREAS

"I found it difficult to stay with the system while disregarding my own feelings. I keep jumping on and off—often just at the wrong time."

~ Ed Seykota

The first part of the plan is to identify any issues that arise in your trading. A self-review each day or week can give you the space to see what you have been doing right and wrong. If your performance has not been up to scratch, then you want to make sure you notice it. Self-awareness is one of the first things you need to trade well.

#2 SPECIFIC WORK AROUND PROBLEMS

"Upon analysis, a trader may find that if he only concentrates on the trades that do well and let's go of the other trades, he might actually be successful."

~ Randy McKay

Generally, the most difficult part will be identifying any issues you may have. Once you know you have a problem, you can then go about seeking a solution. That is, except if you have what Van calls "emotional charge" attached to the issue. For example, if you have an inability to cut your losses short, it may be due to interference from a part of you that is trying to protect you. If that part is interfering unconsciously, it might quite happily stop once it is made aware that it is not actually helping. But if that part was formed in a painful period of your life, it might resist change and continue to hinder your performance.

If this is the case, you may need to do some clearing work. To learn more about this, you can read *Trading Beyond the Matrix*, or complete Van's Peak Performance Course, which also has a home-study version. I include a summary description of some of the exercises below.

#3 WORKING ON THE FOUNDATION

"I spend my day trying to make myself as happy and relaxed as I can be."

~ Paul Tudor Jones

"Don't be a hero. Don't have an ego."

~ Paul Tudor Jones

You want to be consistently clearing the blockages to your true self and eliminating any negative emotions that arise. To do this, make a regular practice of some of the exercises such as meditation or the Course in Miracles. These practices will also serve to strengthen your connection with your Divine.

#4 TECHNICAL WORK AND MARKET KNOWLEDGE

"It's a matter of both having confidence and being comfortable in the approach you're using."

~ Tom Basso

Part of your self-development plan should be to improve any technical aspects that need work. Perhaps you do not implement your ideas with the degree of accuracy you would like, or you don't understand how to use risk/reward ratios or R-multiples. Maybe your system is not achieving the desired results and needs improving.

#5 THE TRADING TRIBE PROCESS AND COACHING

Market Wizard Ed Seykota believes in the value of having a "support group" to help you with your trading. One such group is The Trading Tribe. In his words:

"The Trading Tribe is an association of people who commit to excellence, personal growth and supporting and receiving support from each other."

In your development plan, include how you will network with traders who will help you with your trading. Market Wizard Ari Kiev also places a large store of value in having the support and accountability of a trading group. You might also consider coaching. Trading is a high-performance endeavor, and just like in other similar high-performance fields, coaching can be a big help.

HIGH-VALUE ACTIVITIES FOR TRADERS

"I think investment psychology is by far the most important element, followed by risk control, with the least important consideration being the question of where you can buy and sell."

~ Tom Basso

The following is a list of activities that are targeting change on a deep level and come highly recommended to traders.

Important Note: Most of these are Van Tharp's suggestions.

INTERFERENCE, PARTS INTEGRATION

When you have parts that are causing you issues, you can engage with them, and look to integrate them into your "Divine". Instead of being a mess of conflicting parts, you start to become a whole.

EMOTIONS, FEELING RELEASE

If you have strong emotions, the temptation is either to resist them or to distract yourself from them (by TV, eating, sex, etc.). Instead of resisting the emotion, one technique is to find a quiet space, and really try your hardest to feel it. Once you stop resisting and really start to feel, it can cause the emotion to lose its charge and dissipate.

GRATITUDE, THE MAGIC

Gratitude is the secret ingredient to trading success that Van Tharp urges traders to practice. Rhonda Byrne's book, *The Magic*, contains twenty-eight days of exercises designed to apply gratitude to your everyday life.

PERCEPTIONS, COURSE IN MIRACLES

The *Course in Miracles* contains three hundred and sixty-five daily lessons designed to create major transformation in your life. This course has a religious background, but don't throw the baby out with the bathwater if this is not something you would normally do.

WEALTH, THE ABUNDANCE BOOK

Many people have issues around lacking wealth, and the forty-day program in the *Abundance* book is designed to clear out any negativity toward wealth and help you to create abundance in your life.

MENTALITY, READ *THE MARKET WIZARDS* BOOKS

Reading the four *Market Wizards* books will give you an insight into the minds of history's greatest traders. You can read them several times, and you will learn new insights when you read them with fresh eyes.

QUIETING THE MIND, MEDITATION

The daily practice of mediation is like exercise for the mind. The more you meditate, the more you will notice that your emotional capacity increases. Things that used to bother you start to seem trivial, and you become happier and more peaceful in general.

THOUGHTS THAT CAUSE ANGER AND FEAR, THE WORK

The Work, by Byron Katie, is an easy-to-use exercise that helps you deal with thoughts that cause blockages to your true self. It is a good exercise to do with other family members.

CHANGE CAN HAPPEN OVERNIGHT

"The key to trading success is emotional discipline. Making Money has nothing to do with intelligence."

~ *Victor Sperandeo*

Self-work is an on-going process. Once you get started, you will never stop!

But the good news is that change can happen overnight. If you have an issue you are able to effectively identify and deal with, then your progress can be very quick. In *Market Wizards*, Van Tharp gives several examples of exercises that cleared significant blockages in the course of a day, with a week or two of follow-up integration. This is particularly true if the changes happen at the foundations.

Get started writing a simple self-development plan, and choose one or two exercises to begin with this week. Those few moments a day you take to work on yourself could not only change your trading but your life—so don't wait!

How to Get in the Trading Zone Like an Elite Athlete

"Complex activities are best performed with only a moderate amount of emotional arousal."

~ Ari Kiev

To trade effectively, you need to learn to function in a tense, unstructured, and unpredictable trading environment. In this type of environment, a lack of focus, indecisiveness, and a preoccupation with past (or future) failures are all significant impediments to performance. Rather, traders function better when they are in the zone—a state of intense clarity in the present moment, from which they emanate confidence (but not arrogance).

Getting in the zone is not something that magically occurs when your luck is in. It can be done regularly with the proper mental and physical preparation. Like an elite athlete preparing for a gold-medal race, being a top trader requires hard work and the right mental strategies.

Stress Management for Traders

"If stress increases without a corresponding increase in your ability to handle it, your adaptive mechanisms begin to break down, and you experience nervousness and decreased confidence."

~ Ari Kiev

When you feel anxious or depressed about your trading, it is your thoughts producing a stress response in your body. This is a biological activation of the pituitary and adrenal glands, the thymus, the hypothalamus, and the thyroid system. It is a physical reaction to your thoughts in relation to traumatic experiences (such as a previous loss, or your perception of a future loss). These bodily triggers cause emotions that can interfere with—or worse, hijack—the decision-making process. They are also the enemy of a receptive state of mind, as the focus shifts to the stress event and ignores the full spectrum of input the trader could and should be experiencing.

Needless to say, a highly stressed trader is going to have trouble getting into the zone. In fact, stress does not exist when the trader is totally focused on the moment. Stress arises out of thinking about the past or future, both of which do not exist in the *now*.

GOAL SETTING AS A PERFORMANCE TOOL

"It is a little bit like playing golf: You can throw the clubs around after making a bad shot, but while you are making the next shot you should keep your head down and your eye on the ball."

~ Richard Dennis

In chapter 3, we talked about goal setting as a step in defining your position-sizing model, calculating your approach to the markets, and to help you get clear about what you really want out of life and trading.

In this lesson, goal setting is a critical management tool used to direct both your creativity and focus in the pursuit of achieving a near-term stretch goal. You select a daily, weekly, or monthly goal that deep down you believe you can achieve, in line with your current methodology and financial resources. You then devise a strategy to achieve that goal. You learn to isolate and pay sharp attention to the most critical elements of achieving your goal, and to eliminate non-core activity.

STRETCH GOALS HELP YOU DEFINE THE STRATEGY THAT IT TAKES TO WIN

"If you reach high, you might just amaze yourself."

~ Richard Driehaus

"The goal medal winners are always stretching for a goal that is uncertain."

~ *Ari Kiev*

By giving yourself an aspirational goal, you stretch your mind and challenge yourself to figure out how you are going to get what you want from the markets. This is why a goal that does not push you generally fails to produce the results you are after.

Market Wizard and trading psychologist Ari Kiev relates a story in which a young skating star's coach was undecided if he should push for a gold medal in the up-coming world championship, or focus on the more distant Olympics. He was worried about the impact that a failure to succeed in the world championships might have on the youngster. Kiev urged the coach to go for the gold in the nearer event but to make sure he came up with a strategy that if executed could achieve the goal. This involved learning new skating skills and a new demeanor for his skater, who was known as an "ice queen". The first step is committing to the vision, and the second step is to organize a strategy for realizing it, suggests Kiev.

Traders should continually ask themselves what it is they need to do to produce the results they hunger for. How can they get better or more ideas? What information do they need to formulate a variant perception? What can they do that would give them the confidence to take bigger positions? What is missing from their strategy that is holding it back from achieving their goals?

THE GOAL SETTER'S PARADOX

"To express your vision from within your creative self, you need to let go of your concerns moment by moment and stop trying to manage the future. You should focus only on what you can do in the next moment... stay present to the moment before you, and, in time (much to your amazement), you will find yourself in the process of actualizing yourself – becoming what you have set out to become."

~ *Ari Kiev*

After the goal and the strategy to achieve the goal are established, detachment from the goal becomes necessary. This is the goal setter's paradox. Once a goal is established, top traders use it as a guide to assess and evaluate the effectiveness of their actions in the now. You want to focus your energy, attention, and drive on the actions that are critical to achievement of the goal but not the goal itself. To illustrate this point, Kiev uses an example from a book called *Zen in the Art of Archery*:

"[The Author]... studied with a master in Japan for five years. At the end of his time in Japan he realized that he didn't even have to look at the target, since it wasn't about hitting the target. He can hit the target with his eyes closed. It's all about being in the right position internally and allowing the arrow to be released from the pull-back position without putting any consciousness on the release of the arrow. You let go of the arrow and it surprises you. It goes without anything impinging on the arrow to misdirect it."

If you focus on the process behind the goal, you can achieve your goal simply as a by-product of mastering the process. The goal is the roadmap that helps you notice if your processes are on track or not; your attachment to the goal starts and ends there. A focus on the goal itself generates emotional responses that impinge on its achievement.

FINDING YOUR CENTER

"I feel like a ninja in a fight. In other words, when it comes at you, it seems like slow motion. OK, it is what it is. Because there's a calmness. So when there's a calmness, I can deal with it in a better way. Whereas, when there's that anxiety, it all seems so fast and less I am in control."

~ Ray Dalio

"Previous hands mean nothing."

~ Mark Minervini

Being able to give yourself to trading in the fullest most present sense while remaining relaxed is the cornerstone mental state for trading. You are in the zone, totally focused on the current moment—free from the negativity that arises from past losses or anxiety from a future expectation. This state allows for clarity in the decision-making process, non-consensus thinking, and immediate action during high-pressure situations.

This is true of both day traders who are stalking opportunities over the short-term and long-term traders who are looking for conviction about their positions or for new ideas to deploy their capital. Again, Kiev uses the example of an elite athlete to illustrate this point. After the slow start to his career that almost saw baseball legend Sadaharu Oh warming the bench for his team, the Tokyo Giants, he met a master who encouraged him to discover his "ki". or his center, when batting. Once he integrated this practice into his batting, he went on to become the all-time career record holder for home runs hit in the history of baseball.

RELAXATION IS THE KEY

"Meditation, more than any other factor, has been the reason for what success I've had."

~ Ray Dalio

Tension is the enemy of the trader looking to enter the zone. Tension gives you blinkers that hamper creativity and cause mistakes. In contrast, a relaxed state of mind, in which you simply and humbly respond to events, as per your plan, is much more effective for trading.

There are plenty of techniques that can help you relax, including meditation, contemplation of a phrase or idea, physical relaxation through Yoga, and many others. It will be a matter of personal preference, time, and resources as to which method you choose.

What's important is not so much the method but the "empty minded" state that relaxation helps you to achieve. You want your mind quiet and focused on the task at hand. In that state, any tension you feel will dissolve. You will find that, until you are well practiced, you will catch your mind wandering. That is okay. Don't judge yourself; instead, bring your mind gently back to the task at hand. Don't try to resist any discomfort. Rather, coolly detach and observe it as an objective outsider to your mind. Practice the relaxed state as much as possible. If you are doing the dishes, then do them calmly and consciously. If you are taking the dog for a walk, notice what is going on around you. Exist in the moment, not in your past or future. Work hard to eliminate any sources of stress from your life.

DO THE PREPARATION WORK

"It is a question of being prepared, having a game plan, having an ability to react to market movements. It is like tennis. You have to know where your racquet is and keep your eye on the ball and then maximize the performance by playing intuitively."

~ Ari Kiev

To use another sporting example, master cricket batsman Ricky Ponting would say to himself "watch the ball" as the bowler ran in to deliver it. By focusing on that one simple mantra, all distraction and preoccupation with his batting technique would disappear. His training would kick in, and he would play the ball on its merits.

The important point here is that Ponting had prepared himself so well for whatever type of ball was bowled at him, that he was able to completely exist in the moment with it. If Ponting had walked out to the pitch ill-prepared for what was going to come his way, then no matter how much he focused on the ball, he would not have the skills to handle a cricket ball coming his way at 140-150K an hour. Similarly, if he was overly preoccupied with his technique, the hundred runs he wants to get, or the duck he got last innings, then all the preparation in the world is not going to help him.

It is the same for traders. You need to have done the homework that gives you the conviction in your ideas to be able to execute them, and then have the consciousness not to make emotional mistakes.

DEVELOP MASTERY OF YOUR CORE TRADING SKILLS

"People ask me all the time, 'How long do you think it will take for me to succeed?' I tell them 'three to five years of twelve-hour days and losing money'. Very few people want to hear that."

~Mark Cook

Vince Lombardi is one the most renowned NFL football coaches of all time. He won five NFL play-offs in the space of seven years and never coached a team with a losing record. He did this all by pursuing a relentless focus on the basics. He started the 1961 Green Bay Packers' training camp with the most elementary statement of all—"This is a football"—and held up a pigskin ball. The Green Bay Packers had lost the final in the last season by squandering a 4th quarter lead to the Philadelphia Eagles—they were not a bunch of raw recruits. During the year, his team joked with him that he was going too fast for them when he was making them work on perfecting the tasks players at this level usually took for granted. In 1961, the Green Bay Packers won the Super Bowl by 37-0.

As a trader, perfect execution of the basic trading skills will generate your results. Not increasingly complex techniques or theories. The markets are simple, in that the price moves up and down and sometimes trends. It forms chart patterns based on human psychology and responds to fundamental developments in the country of that currency.

Practice sizing your positions in-line with your conviction, cutting your losses short, letting your profits run, and being receptive to the information the market provides you. Time spent mastering these basics will be much better than studying Elliot Wave Theory, Fibonacci levels, or other esoteric trading approaches. It's far better to ingrain the basics in your subconscious, so you perform them automatically without a moment's hesitation or thought, even during situations that generate extreme levels of stress.

Note: I'm not saying Elliot Wave, etc., are not useful tools for analyzing the market, and I don't what to alienate traders who believe in them. They can be handy models of the market, and several good traders I know use these techniques well. Just know that you will get better results by focusing your energy on the more important core skills.

USE VISUALIZATION AND MENTAL-REHEARSAL TECHNIQUES FOR PERFECT PRACTICE

"Mental rehearsal will go a long way toward improving performance."

~ Van Tharp

Visualization and mental-rehearsal techniques are very useful tools for traders looking to get in the zone. Van Tharp relates the story of the US Army's top two snipers. Both were incredibly accurate shots, and both believed in mentally rehearsing their performance prior to putting their skills to use on the shooting range.

But one sniper in the pair always out-performed the other in shoots. One of the differences (if not the core difference) between the best shooter and his off-sider was in the way they visually rehearsed for the event the night before. The second-best shooter would visualize himself hitting the bullseye with each shot. In contrast, the top performing shooter would not only visualize himself hitting the bullseye as he fired his shot but hitting the very center of the bullseye. He also believed he needed to practice the entire one thousand-round event in his mind the night before, as opposed to practicing a few times as the second best shooter did.

Van also tells the story of a professional cyclist who was worried about a certain dangerous situation occurring that had seriously injured a friend of his. This particular scenario was not something he could practice in real life. So to safeguard himself, he formulated a plan about what he would do if it occurred, and he rehearsed it several times in his mind.

One day, about a year later, he was involved in the situation he feared, and he reacted in exactly the way he had rehearsed, by flipping the bike out from under him and landing on his feet. This pre-programmed reaction saved him from serious injury, and simply would not have been in his resources if he had not prepared thoroughly beforehand.

Similar to the examples above, traders can use visualization techniques to mentally rehearse both the perfect execution of their trading plan and their response to a situation where one of their contingency plans need to come into play. When doing this as a trader, it is important not only to plan how to manage risk but how you can potentially capitalize on a scenario.

THE TAO OF FOREX TRADING

"I focus my total attention on trading well, and let the results take care of themselves."

~ Tom Basso

Take a moment, and imagine you are relaxed, calm, and centered. Aware of yet detached from your goal. You have a clearly defined plan to achieve your goal, and you have all your mental resources at your disposal because you know exactly how to handle stress.

Now imagine you are also able to implement your core trading skills unconsciously and automatically, without a moment's hesitation. Imagine you have practiced the perfect execution of your plan thousands of times in your mind's eye.

Finally, add to that, you have practiced hundreds of times what you will do if one of your contingency plans needs to be executed, and you feel ready for anything the market might throw at you.

Now hold on to that mental picture, and answer this question: How well do you think you would trade?

Constructing Advanced Position-Sizing Algorithms to Achieve Your Trading Goals

Let's take a trip back in time a few weeks.

In chapter 6, we talked about the importance of setting objectives for your trading, and then in chapter 7, we discussed how you achieve these objectives through your position-sizing model. But building a position-sizing model should not necessarily be that simple. There are two areas where complexity can significantly boost trading performance: in your exits and your position sizing. If you get it right, your position-sizing model can offer a powerful boost to your trading system's performance.

In addition, your model plays an important part in your risk-management plan. If it is not robustly designed, then any number of unlikely but very possible scenarios could have a devastating impact on your account's equity. In this chapter, we will look at how you can use advanced position-sizing algorithms to maximize your returns.

If you have not mastered the concepts in chapters 5, 6, and 7, please go back and review them now. For deeper coverage of some of the topics in both chapter 7 and this chapter, I suggest you read Van Tharp's *Definitive Guide to Position Sizing Strategies*. Much of the subject matter in this post is inspired by the *Definitive Guide*.

Different Types Of R Multiples

"Always define an exit point before you enter a position."

~ Van Tharp

Back in chapter 5, we introduced the concept of R-multiples. R-multiples are a method of defining your initial risk, developed by Van K. Tharp. If you risk $100 on a trade, you are risking 1R for example.

Thus, $200 would be 2R. This is a more detached way of looking at profit versus risk.

Van also provides some additional ways of classifying R that are useful:

- Risk per unit (Ru). When trading currencies, this is your initial risk in pips. For example, your initial risk might be 100 pips on a trade, so your Ru would be 100 pips.

- Total risk (Rt). This is your initial risk times your total quantity. So if you traded at a size of $50,000 and risked 100 pips, your Rt would be $500 (If you purchase $50,000 of currency, you are risking roughly $5 per pip. If your stop-loss is 100 pips away, your total risk would be 100 x$5 or $500).

There is more than one definition of R-multiples, so be aware of this when the concept is discussed. In particular, traders will often be referring to Ru when discussing R-multiples.

GROUP CONTROL, MANAGING CORRELATIONS IN FOREX

"My money management was poor. I had too many correlated trades."

~ *Bruce Kovner*

One of the major position-sizing errors made by Forex traders using a multi-pair system is failing to take correlations into account. No currency is an island. You may find that all your USD trades go against you at one time for example. Note that the relationship between currency pairs changes, depending on the timeframe your data is across. Also note that some positions are inversely correlated, meaning they tend to move in opposite directions to each other.

Correlations make selecting your system's pairs critical to how you construct your position-sizing algorithm. If you want to hold multiple correlated currency pairs, then you may need to trade smaller sizes than if you hold a limited number of less-correlated instruments.

One way of doing this is to limit the percentage of open risk per group of correlated markets to a set amount, such as 3%. Other traders choose to focus on a smaller basket of currency pairs as their method of managing correlations.

This is where it can be useful to add markets outside of Forex—such as indices and commodities—to your basket of traded markets. But remember, there is no guarantee that an index or commodity is not correlated with a currency pair.

PORTFOLIO HEAT

"The moral is you have to know your net exposure comfort zone."

~ Jack Schwager

Even if you think you are trading a number of non-correlated markets, when things turn to custard, you might find that everything starts to move against you at one time. The concept of portfolio heat protects you during this type of scenario.

Your portfolio heat is the amount of risk your portfolio of trades has at any one time. For example, if you have five trades on, all risking 2%, then your portfolio heat would be 10% (5 x 2%).

The amount of risk you have in your portfolio should be dependent on the quality of your trading system. If you have a poor-quality system and have 20-30% of your equity at risk at one time, you are asking for trouble. But if you have an excellent system that is run across a number of non-correlated markets, with a limited amount of leverage, then this level of risk could be acceptable.

As a general rule, most systems should not have a portfolio heat above 15%. If you are inexperienced or risking your core capital—as opposed to your profits—then you will want to have significantly less than this.

THE IMPORTANCE OF UNDERSTANDING YOUR SYSTEM

"One of the fundamentals that you as a trader must know is how to evaluate the effectiveness of your trading methodology."

~ Van Tharp

The better you understand the distribution of R-multiples your system produces, the better you will be able to size your positions. Your R-multiple distribution is simply what a series of trades might look like. For example, over 100 trades you might expect to have 40 -1R trades, 8 -2R trades, 2 -5R trades, 25 1R trades, 15 2R trades, 8 5R trades and 2 10R trades.

Armed with this information, along with your objectives, you can run functional simulations of your trading system. If you risk different amounts and record the results, you can come close to finding an optimal amount to risk per trade to produce the best returns. Alternatively, for the discretionary trader (who does not have access to a simulator), this information will help you to make more informed decisions about how to size your positions. You can then run manual tests using Van Tharp's position-sizing game (available on his website).

THE BETTER YOUR SYSTEM, THE MORE YOU CAN RISK

"Position sizing is not only in avoiding trading too large, but in trading larger when warranted."

~ Jack Schwager

While it is important to understand the distribution of R-multiple results your system returns, it is also important to understand the quality of your system. Simply put: the better your system, the more you can afford to risk per trade.

You can determine the quality of your system. Van Tharp has developed what he terms a system quality number (SQN). How the SQN is derived can be found in the *Definitive Guide to Position Sizing*. The greater the SQN, the more you can feel comfortable risking on each trade. The good news is the folks at Tradervue will automatically calculate this for you based on your system's performance if you use their reporting software.

Irrespective of if you use SQN or not to grade your system, the better the system, the greater you can size the position.

MANAGING OPEN RISK (RISK ON PROFITS)

If you trade effectively, especially if you use a scale-in technique, at some point, you will end up with a large open profit. While this is a nice scenario to get into, holding on to your profits requires careful management. One news event and all your hard-earned profits could be wiped out.

Because of this, you may need some rules in your position-sizing algorithm that help you make sure you hold on to your profit. Without these, you could see some wild swings in your account. To do this, you could allocate a maximum R drawdown you are willing to experience in a trade. Alternatively, you could use a trailing stop that serves to achieve the same thing.

You may also want to have this rule based on a group of trades, or account wide. For example, if your account has a 3R drawdown in profits across multiple positions, you might start to trim back all your positions. Or you may have a rule that once you have achieved a certain amount of profit, you become less willing to withstand a drawdown (maybe your trailing stop becomes 2 or 1.5R rather than 3). This is simply prudence in trading at work.

POSITION SIZING BASED ON MARKET OR TRADE TYPE

"Traders need to adjust position size in response to the changing market environment."

~ Jack Schwager

You may use different position sizes based on the type of trade you are looking to place. For example, if you have a portfolio that contains a mix of short and long-term positions, you generally will want to have different sizes for each. For example, you might risk 0.3-0.5% of your account on a short-term position, but risk 1-2% on longer-term trades. In addition, you may decide to trade smaller in sideways market types and larger in trending markets. Or perhaps you choose not to scale-in during sideways market types. Remember to fit the right position-sizing approach to your strategy.

NEWS EVENT MANAGEMENT

The currency markets can be significantly volatile around news events. Sometimes days or even weeks of profit can disappear in a heartbeat. On the plus side, since you know the event is coming, you can prepare for it. If a potentially volatile event is on the horizon, then you have a few options.

- Trim your position size.

- Place a stop on your position close to the market in case it goes against you.

- Protect part or all of your position with options.

- Use short-term options that win if your position moves rapidly against you.

Often a combination of some or all of the above will work best. Think about your objectives and how much you are willing to give back if the market does move against you.

POSITION SIZING ON YOUR INITIAL CORE CAPITAL

"The most important thing is to keep enough powder for a comeback."

~ Marty Schwatrz

If you don't protect your trading capital, you will be out of the game. Many traders start out by risking large chunks of their own funds. But what they don't know is that when they first start trading is the time they are most likely to lose. Instead, you should have a position-sizing model you use on your core capital to protect it in the initial stages, before your normal position-sizing model kicks in.

Generally, you want to keep the risk as small as possible when you begin, and then once you have profit, you can start to trade at a larger size. For example, if your normal position-sizing model calls for you to risk 1% on a trade, you might risk 0.2% of your core capital, just to start with. Once your core capital is up 1 or 2%, you might then start to risk 0.4%, and so on, until you are well into profit. This serves to protect your capital when it is at its most vulnerable, and it gives you the best chance to become a winner.

THE COURAGE TO BE A PIG, CONVICTION-BASED POSITION SIZING

"If a trader does better on high confidence trades, then the degree of confidence can serve as a proxy for probability of winning. The implication then becomes to trade larger on high confidence trades and smaller, or not at all, on low confidence trades."

~ Jack Schwager

Conviction-based position sizing is often what separates a great trader from a mediocre one, (and great returns from mediocre ones). Your good ideas should make a lot more than your mediocre ones. But most position-sizing models don't offer a great framework for this type of approach. Your high-conviction trades might merit a leverage of several times your account size and a level of risk far greater than a typical trade. Generally, you don't want to build to this level of risk all in one go. You may want to use a scale-in approach as outlined in chapter 13. As the trade goes for you, add more size. When you build your position-sizing model, keep this as systematic as possible, while giving yourself room to trust your judgment.

WATCH YOUR EGGS CLOSELY

Stanley Druckenmiller does not believe in diversification as it is taught in business school. He would instead prefer to put all his eggs in one basket, and watch them closely. This approach leads to some spectacular returns. If you had invested $1000 with Druckenmiller at the start of his career, it would be worth $2.6 million now. In addition, he has never had a losing year in his career.

You may find this 2015 interview of Druckenmiller well worth the read.

USING ACCOUNT-BASED GOALS

Some traders prefer to adjust their position-sizing model based on where they are at throughout the month or year. Marty Schwartz would "be poor in January", effectively starting from scratch each year. At the start of each year, all his money is "core capital", which he is miserly with. Once in profit for the year, he expands his position sizing.

Similarly, Stanley Druckenmiller seeks to grind out the first part of the year until he is up by 30%. Once he has hit that level, he will then start to trade much bigger on his high-conviction ideas. Creating milestones like this can be a powerful tool to help you generate outsized returns while limiting risk.

MARKET'S MONEY

We touched on market's money in chapter 7, but the topic is worth expanding on here. Market's money is possibly the best way to increase your returns, so it's very important for the trader to learn different ways of employing it, so they can best fit it to their strategy.

CLOSED TRADE VS. OPEN TRADE

"Once he is ahead on the trade, he will allow for more risk latitude. This approach all but ensures losses on new trades are likely to be moderate."

~ Jack Schwager, discussing Market Wizard Scott Ramsey

The first distinction to make when planning to use market's money is to consider whether you will use market's money during a trade (i.e. scaling in). Maybe you'd prefer to apply it to your account over a set time period. For example, if you are up 5% for the month, you may decide to risk more on your next trades. You have a choice of using either, or you could combine the two, and scale-in aggressively when your account is already in a profit for the time period.

WHEN DOES MARKET'S MONEY BECOME CORE CAPITAL?

Your next consideration is to decide when market's money is "banked" and becomes core capital. At some point, you will want to lock in the profits you have made. The timing will depend on your objectives, though a common way to do it would be over a time period, such as a week, month, or year. Alternatively, it could be based on some form of return goal.

A VARIATION OF THE MARKET MONEY APPROACH, TWO POTS

In the *Definitive Guide to Position Sizing*, Van Tharp outlines a variation of the market's money approach he terms "two pots". When employing the two-pot approach, a trader would add a percentage of their profits to a separate account, which is treated as market's money. For example, 20% of the profits on a trade might go into another account that aggressively targets large gains, while the other 80% is treated as core capital and traded conservatively.

USING MARKET'S MONEY TO CREATE AN ASYMMETRICAL RISK PROFILE DURING A TRADE

"It helps greatly to have a long-term objective that you have derived by really doing your homework. You combine the long-term objective with the protective stop that you move as the position goes your way."

~ Gary Bielfeldt

If you add to your position once you are in profit and then combine the stop on the positions, you can have the effect of creating a position where the risk is limited to the downside, but the profit potential is significant, whilst still maintaining a wide stop.

Let me use an example of a longer-term trade on the EURUSD.

On this trade, we are looking for 1000 pips with a 300-pip stop-loss, giving a risk/reward ratio of 3.3:1. Let's see how this trade was converted into one that could generate 15 times your risk or more, using market's money and a scale-in approach (a risk reward of 15:1).

Firstly, you still want to stalk a good entry. It will improve your success rate and the risk/reward even more. Preferably, you also want a catalyst that triggers the trade. When you get your entry signal, establish your initial position as you would normally—but make sure you keep your stop-loss well out of the way of any noise. Try tripling what you normally use.

As the market goes for you, scale in to an additional position. You will want it to have gone another 100-150 pips. Preferably, you want to stalk another good entry point for the new position. When you add the additional position, combine the stops, and move them up jointly so you are risking no more than the original amount of money. In other words, if you were risking 2% of your account, then move the stop until you are still risking no more than 2% on the combined position.

As you had some profit from the first position, you will still be able to maintain a wide stop, even though your position size is twice as large. If you set a new profit target for 1000 pips on the additional position, then you have the same risk of 2% of your account, but you stand to make an additional 3.3R on the trade. Your risk reward is 6.6:1 now.

You can put the profit target on the second position at the same place as the original position if you like. But having only one profit target is trying to be right about the exit. Better to have multiple targets and other exit rules that cater to changing market conditions (not all trades go as swimmingly well as this one).

Once you have added the second position, keep adding as the price goes for you until you reach your maximum position size. For example, on a trade like this, you might look to add up to five positions as it goes for you. Each new position gives you an additional 3.3 to your risk/reward, without increasing your maximum risk of 2% of your account.

Can you see how this method of position sizing using market's money allows you to generate large gains while still limiting the risk to your core capital?

THE STEP METHOD

Another way to use market's money to scale-in to positions is the step method. As opposed to the above approach of combining your stop-loss, with the step method each new position has a separate stop-loss. But at the same time, the stop-loss orders on the earlier positions are trailed higher, limiting the risk. For example, you might start by risking 0.5% on your first position, then, as it goes into profit, you add a new position, risking another 0.5%. You then move the stop on the original position higher, so your overall risk would be 0.75%. You can then continue to add to the trade until you reach your maximum risk limit. Using this technique, you both:

- Keep losses small if the trend does not eventuate.

- Build a large position while limiting the potential risk.

You also have a variety of stop-losses, so even if one position gets stopped out, you will still have some skin in the game in case the market goes for you.

243

POSITION SIZING FOR DAY TRADING, BULLET METHOD

In the fast-paced world of day trading, if you are not switched on mentally or the market conditions are unfavorable to your strategy, you can lose large sums very quickly. To counter this, day traders should have very strict rules, including:

- Maximum number of positions they can take in a day.

- Maximum number of positions they can hold at any one time.

- Maximum loss in a day before they stop trading.

Ken Long, an instructor from the Van Tharp institute with a military background, developed a position-sizing model designed to achieve this, called the "bullet method".

Ken divides his risk capital into several bullets, which he can fire each day. To do this, you split your daily risk capital into several parts (or bullets), and that is the number of trades you can place in that day. For example, if you were prepared to risk a maximum of 1.5% of your capital, and you wanted to place three trades a day, you might risk 0.5% on each trade.

Of course, you can get quite intricate with how you apply this approach. You may decide to replenish your bullets if you have a winning trade; or, if you have two losing trades, you might split your remaining bullet in half, so you have two smaller trades you can place. You could also use bullets to scale-in to profitable positions or for any other purpose that fits your personality and trading style.

ALLOCATING CAPITAL ACROSS MULTIPLE SYSTEMS

In time, you will want a number of trading systems that work across a variety of strategies, timeframes, and markets (Forex, commodities, stocks, etc.). There are several position-sizing considerations when you run multiple strategies:

- Objectives of the system. You may decide to allocate more to a conservative, long-term growth strategy than to an aggressive system for example.

- The amount of leverage required. Some systems will require more leverage than others, which could be a factor in your allocation.

- Correlations across the systems. Some systems may be correlated or even hold the same currency pair at the same time.

- The SQN of each system. You may want to allocate more to higher-quality systems.

- The maximum drawdown of each system. You may want to allocate more capital to a system with a lower drawdown.

- The holding period of each system (daily, weekly, monthly). A day-trading, discretionary system may require less capital than a long-term, trend-following system.

- The recent performance of each system. If a system is going through a rough patch, you may increase or decrease its capital allocation, depending on its recovery profile.

- The current market type. Some systems don't work as well in certain market types. You may decide to increase or decrease your allocation to certain systems in unfavorable market types (this includes decreasing it to zero).

TO REBALANCE OR NOT TO REBALANCE

In the *Definitive Guide to Position Sizing*, Van Tharp covers the results of a study on rebalancing done by Market Wizard Tom Basso, which was then critiqued by Jack Schwager (the author of the *Market Wizards* books).

Schwager found that if he rebalanced five non-correlated systems monthly, by taking from the winners and adding to the losers, it improved the performance of the systems by reducing the overall drawdown (but not necessarily by increasing returns). However, extrapolating from Basso's earlier study, if the systems show a degree of correlation, then taking from the winner to add to the loser is not a successful approach.

SPEND YOUR ENERGY HERE

"Most people have psychological biases that cause them to want to understand the markets, predict the markets, and be right in their trading. As a result, they totally ignore what is important—cutting their losses short and letting their profits run."

~ *Van Tharp*

As you can see, when you start to get sophisticated about your position sizing, you can come up with an infinite combination of algorithms that you can fit to your particular strategy and goals. You will be far better off if you focus the majority of your attention and energy on designing your position-sizing model, and keep most other aspects of your trading to the side. In terms of importance, it is right up there with psychology.

If you get this wrong, you are setting yourself up for major losses, but if you get it right, you can magnify the performance of your trading system significantly. So forget your charts and news, and dive deep into your position-sizing model. You won't regret it.

THE DAILY TASKS OF MASTER TRADERS

"The really best traders don't think twice about how many hours they're working or whether they come in on a weekend. There is no substitute for that level of commitment."

~ Bill Lipschitz

Becoming a top trader is a journey. There are years of struggle and hard work ahead for most aspiring traders. You will get your butt kicked by the market again and again (most likely just after you thought you had finally "got it"), and you will eventually get to your goal only through dogged determination and sheer willpower. But the good news is it's a battle you can win, and when you do, the carrot is a big one.

In this chapter, we review a daily trading routine defined by Dr. Van K. Tharp in the 12 Top Tasks of Trading. As military philosopher Sun Tzu said, most battles are won before they are started, in the preparation phase. Trading is no different. Here, you will learn how to combine and condense what you have learned throughout this book into action steps you can follow each day to lead you to trading success.

(*Note:* I have shamelessly borrowed the topic for this chapter—with permission—from Van Tharp and applied it specifically to Forex trading. I view the subject matter as essential to effective trading. Any mistakes or omissions are of course my own.)

HOW THE DAILY TASKS WERE DEVELOPED

"The daily tasks fit the metaphor of a hunter, a predator a warrior."

~ Van Tharp

Van Tharp is considered an expert modeler. Throughout his career, he has isolated the common denominators of success across a broad range of trading styles. This has led him to develop a mental map of the daily activities of the master traders. Often these traders would not consciously realize what they were doing to be successful. They would get up, eat, trade, eat, sleep, etc., as far as they were concerned. But through careful prodding and observation, he would eventually learn the things they did differently from other traders who lost in the market.

Here they are... the Top Tasks of Trading:

1. Daily Self Analysis

2. Daily Mental Rehearsal

3. Focus and Intention

4. Developing a Low-Risk Idea

5. Stalking

6. Action

7. Monitoring

8. Abort

9. Take Profits

10. Daily Debriefing

11. Be Grateful for What Went Right

12. Periodic Review

These tasks should form a daily routine that applies to all traders, no matter the currency pair or timeframe. Long-term traders are not excused, though it does not necessarily need to be a daily affair for you. Those who monitor trades once a week might conduct this process once a week.

TOP TASK #1—SELF ANALYSIS

Your performance as a trader is a direct reflection of your level of self-mastery. The more aware you are, the greater your ability to perform in a challenging market environment. Overly emotional or arrogant traders struggle with their consistency in the markets. They tend to make mistakes and miss opportunities that may come their way. In contrast, a self-aware trader exists in the present moment, free from fear and greed. An aware trader is able to make decisions with an open mind.

The trading day should start with an assessment of your trading state. This could be a period of introspection or meditation, during which you focus inwardly, and notice what is going on internally. It could also be a self-rating process, in which you rank yourself out of 7 (this is the number Van Tharp recommends). If you are either too low or too high, you want to meditate—or center yourself—until you are in a more level state. Ideally, you want to be around a 5.

You may also find that certain "parts" within you will be active on a certain day and interfere with your trading. If you can learn to notice the "thoughts and feelings" of these parts, you can provide the parts with what they need, outside of trading.

Action: Spend 15-30 minutes a day meditating or sitting quietly in introspection. Conduct a self-rating assessment.

TOP TASK #2—MENTAL REHEARSAL

As the market throws a wide variety of circumstances at you, it can be very helpful to mentally rehearse yourself performing perfectly when you trade. This rehearsal could be conducted immediately prior to commencing trading or the night before.

The concept of mental rehearsal is borrowed from high-performance sports, where it was discovered that elite athletes—the very best in their field—would visualize their events in full beforehand. They would conduct perfect practice in their mind's eye, which would result in increased performance during the actual event. This rehearsal allowed them to pre-plan their response to scenarios that would arise, in order to anticipate problems and develop solutions, so the correct reaction became automatic.

Traders should visualize themselves following their rules, coolly and calmly. It can be helpful to take into consideration any upcoming news for the following day. If there is important upcoming news, such as Non-Farm Payrolls, then you should consider rehearsing your plan around this. Rehearse for both the best and worst-case scenarios, and you'll be miles ahead of the crowd if anything unexpected happens. It is beneficial to rehearse your contingency plans (from chapter 14) and how you would take advantage of "black swan" market events.

Action: Rehearse the day's trading 5-10 times—either the night before or immediately prior to trading on the day. If you are a day trader, you might find it worthwhile rehearsing every trade you plan to take.

TOP TASK #3—FOCUS AND INTENTION

Top traders have a razor-sharp focus on those activities that lead to the achievement of their goals. For peak performance, it's critical that traders take a moment to re-orientate themselves toward their goals, and set a positive intention for what they want to achieve from the day's trading. When traders lose sight of their objectives, they often make mistakes, and they tend to cut their winners short or let their losses run based on market noise. In addition, a positive intention clears out negativity and aligns the subconscious mind with what you plan to achieve. You may also find it advantageous to review the summary of your trading philosophy, to keep your trading principles fresh in your mind.

Once you have reviewed the goal, you should not focus on it. Instead, you should relax. Detach from the goal, and direct your attention to the activities you have defined in your trading plan that leads to the achievement of your goal. When you start trading, you want to be in this "zone-type" state.

Action: Review your long-term and short-term goals and your trading philosophy (manifesto). Then set a positive intention for the day's trading. After doing this, take a moment to detach from the goal, and focus on the execution of your plan. When you start to review the market, you will be more apt to retain this "in the zone" state.

TOP TASK #4—DEVELOPING A LOW RISK IDEA

Many traders confuse market analysis with developing a low-risk idea. They spend lots of time and energy analyzing the market then try to "fit" the market into their preconceived notions. Dr. Tharp calls it "building a straw house", which gives the trader comfort but avoids the important issues. Remember your fairy tales—how sturdy is a straw house, really?

The concept of developing a low-risk idea provides a lens, or a framework, around market analysis that is more useful to the trader. Your time analyzing the market has one sole purpose: to find low-risk opportunities to make money. It's not about being right, nor is it about some pretty lines on a chart. As one market wizard said, "Trading is not a bullshit fantasy world."

When you develop a low-risk idea, you are looking for opportunities to place a trade congruent with your position-sizing model. You are looking for a desirable risk/reward. Preferably it will be 3:1 or greater, though this will depend on your trading timeframe.

These ideas will usually be relatively simple, but this doesn't mean they're easy to generate. Coming up with a simple and profitable trade idea can require a variant perception, which in turns takes time and a finely tuned intuition to develop.

Dr. Tharp divides this task into three main sub-tasks:

- Gathering data
- Creative brainstorming
- Determining risk/reward

Gathering data involves getting information from charts, fundamental, or other sources (such as sentiment). Creative brainstorm is about looking for a variant perception from the data. Determining risk/reward is firstly about understanding the opportunity that exists and secondly about working out if a plan can be implemented to capitalize upon the idea in a favorable manner.

Action: Gather relevant data, brainstorm any ideas, determine the risk/reward behind those ideas, and come up with an implementation plan.

TOP TASK #5—STALKING

Once you develop a low-risk idea, you want to act like a hunter stalking your prey. Good traders don't jump right in. Instead, they wait for the optimal time to enter: when the odds are the most in their favor. One market wizard describes himself as a cheetah. Even though cheetahs are one of the fastest animals on Earth, they wait patiently for an easy kill before expending their energy.

Stalking is essentially going to a lower timeframe chart or, as Van puts it, "becoming a day trader" in order to find an entry point that improves the risk/reward, while still allowing you to put your stop-loss in a "hard-to-hit" place. Ideally, you would wait for a catalyst if it has not occurred already. The correct mindset for stalking is calm, detached, and objective. It is highly important that you are in flow with the market and sensitive to meaningful inputs or cues.

Action: Examine lower timeframes for opportunities to improve the risk/reward on your trade, while still maintaining a hard-to-hit stop-loss. Check for fundamental catalysts.

TOP TASK #6—ACTION

Once your conditions for entry have been met, it is time to enter into the trade. Traders who have trouble "pulling the trigger" will be experiencing difficulty with this step. The stalking state of mind is very different from the state of mind needed to take action, and this transition can be difficult for some traders. Taking action requires decisiveness and commitment, and any sort of second-guessing or reflection is inappropriate.

One of the preconditions of the action phase is to feel good about the trade you are going to take. If you don't feel good, then it is difficult to trade. Whether the trade feels hard (against consensus) or easy (with the flock) is almost irrelevant. There is no one-size-fits-all formula. What's important is simply that you feel good about it. A key aspect of this phase is identifying what a high-conviction trade "feels like", so use your trading journal to note your feelings as you trade until you learn what you are feeling on the successful trades.

Once you feel good, then you need to check that you are not making any mistakes on the trading terminal to avoid any losses due to fat fingers. Double check that your position size is accurate, and quickly fix any mistakes if you have made an error.

Action: Feel good about your trade. Check your terminal. Execute your trade. Double-check your position. Quickly fix any mistakes.

TOP TASK #7—MONITORING

I have noticed that the monitoring phase is one that many Forex traders struggle with. They lack a clear plan that includes enough options to handle changing market conditions. This leads them to either wait for their position to hit their stop-loss or profit target, or they exit out of the trade based on an emotional response to market noise. Instead, the master trader carefully monitors their position as it moves toward the objective. Van suggests that monitoring is broken down into two types:

- Overview monitoring
- Detailed monitoring.

OVERVIEW MONITORING

During overview monitoring, the trader steps back and takes a big-picture view of his position. As Van says, "She is looking at the forest instead of a detailed view of the trees." She is sitting back and comparing market events with her plan, looking for insights that indicate a change in the reasons she is in the trade. This could include the market not responding to news how it should, or it could be a change in the price action.

In addition, overview monitoring is a method of risk control. If a trade is going for you, it should be easy to hold on to as it moves in your favor. If it's requiring a lot of detailed monitoring, or the market is not behaving how it should, it is a sign you might want to reduce your position size or get out.

DETAILED MONITORING

At times, you should zero in your focus on the position. When you first get in, you want to make sure the trade does what you expect, and you may quickly choose to get out if the market reverses after your entry.

You may want to conduct detailed monitoring when there is an opportunity to add to the position or if the price approaches a pre-planned exit point. You may decide to hold on to the position, tighten the stop-loss, exit part or all of the position, or a combination of the above. There are also certain risk events you might want to pay particular attention to. If there is a major news event that has the potential to move your position, you might want to plan what to do if it goes against you (or for you). For example, you might want to tighten the stop on part of your position, in case you get news that moves the market rapidly against your trade.

Action: Broaden your focus, and conduct overview monitoring, and where appropriate, zoom in and conduct detailed monitoring.

TOP TASK #8—ABORTING

The abort task is where you either exit out of a position that is moving against you, or where circumstances have changed. Similar to Task 6, this is an "action" phase where decisiveness is required. Your decision about where to exit will be either pre-planned or arise from the monitoring phase. It's where you execute your risk control by cutting losses. According to Van, traders have three beliefs about where to exit:

If the market is going against the trader beyond a threshold as determined by the risk-management plan, then the trader should act and get out.

When the reason for the trade no longer exists, then get out. Additionally, if you feel uncertain about the position, then you might want to take this as a sign to get out. You want to feel conviction in your positions.

If the trade has not moved how you expect within a specified time period, then get out. Van suggests that one of the advantages retail traders have is that you don't have to be in the market if you don't want to be. Only stay with a position when things are stacked up in your favor. Otherwise, close it.

Once you determine, through monitoring, the appropriate time to abort, you then need to change your mental state to one of focus and action, and commit to your decision to close the trade. Of course, you will want to use stop-loss orders and trailing stops as much as possible.

Action: Assess if the position should be aborted, and switch to the right mental state for action...then take action.

TOP TASK #9—TAKE PROFITS

Many traders spend most of their focus on their entry and not when to exit. This means they end up with not as much profit as they should from their winning positions. In addition, many traders over-emphasize being right, and make taking profits an all-or-nothing decision, rather than scaling out of positions once the trade enters a target area. Before you enter into a trade, you should know your profit potential (ideally in terms of risk). With this in mind you should have a number of rules in place that give you the best opportunity to achieve or exceed that profit potential, while managing risk and adapting to changes in market conditions.

Van believes top traders have four primary beliefs about taking profits:

1. Top traders avoid being greedy and simply react to the signals provided by the market.

2. Top traders are patient and allow the market to move toward the objective, though they will get out if things change along the way.

3. If market volatility or risk conditions change dramatically, they will get out.

4. In a climatic market phase, such as bull or bear volatile market types, profits should be taken quickly.

I would also add that top traders don't get overly worried if a move goes much further than their profit objective. Once they are out, they don't chase the market if it continues to trend. Similar to the action and abort tasks, profit taking requires a focused, action-orientated state of mind. This will mean a mental shift from the state of mind you use for monitoring your position once you are ready to take profits.

Action: Monitor for one of your profit-taking conditions to come into play, and switch to an action state of mind in order to execute.

TOP TASK #10—DAILY DEBRIEFING

Daily debriefings facilitate two things. They allow the trader to note any mistakes they may have made, and avoid making them again. They allow the trader to create a record of what works for them in the market, which they can review to develop their trading systems and processes. A daily debriefing does not need to be a time-consuming process. It might be as simple as spending 5-10 minutes writing in your trading journal, or it could involve more in-depth retrospection. Van suggests that, when conducting a daily debriefing, it is important to avoid any type of self-recrimination about mistakes that have been made. That is not helpful behavior. Instead, review the situation, and then develop and rehearse more productive options that might have been available to you.

Action: Debrief your trading each day. Keep notes in your trading journal.

TOP TASK #11—BE GRATEFUL FOR WHAT WENT RIGHT

The practice of giving thanks is a later addition to Van's top tasks of trading. Van spent a lot of time keeping a journal of the issues he faced every day in order to "clear" them. While this can be useful to do, after some time, he realized he was spending much of his energy finding problems, so they could be cleared. Instead, he started to look for the blessings in his life. What gradually happened was a lightening of his spirit. He started to ask traders to apply this practice each day when they traded—to dramatic effect.

Whether it is the law of attraction in action or simply an excellent method of staying humble, it is a good way to shift the trader's state of mind to the positive (much better for trading than being negative). Whichever way it works, it is an important part of the top traders' routine.

Action: Spend a moment each day writing down what you are grateful for.

TOP TASK #12—PERIODIC REVIEW

As the markets change, so do you.

By conducting an objective review of both the appropriateness of your trading rules and yourself, you ensure you adapt to an ever-changing market environment. While the periodic review is not conducted daily, it is listed by Van as one of the core tasks of top traders. You should establish a routine, depending on how frequently you trade, which allows you to sit back and take an objective look at what you do. The more you trade, the more often you need to complete the review process.

The review process should include:

- Going through your writings from your debriefings.

- Reviewing your trading plan, business plan, and manifesto.

- Reviewing your individual performance and what you have learned.

Van suggests you should spend at least a day on the periodic review.

Action: Depending on how often you trade, conduct a review of both your trading plan and yourself.

THE POINTY END

As we come to the pointy end of this book, you will be starting to integrate everything you have learned into cohesive action steps for you to take every day that you trade. My hope is that now you can see how each chapter fits together and how they all work together in the daily tasks to generate wealth from the market.

By following the twelve top tasks, you are applying the daily practices of master traders. Master traders don't just know the markets, they know themselves. They know precisely how each and every part of their personality comes together to produce results. They know when they're in the zone, and, more importantly, they know how to get there when they're not. They know how to hold themselves under a microscope. They know how to take profits, cut losses, and preserve capital. On the whole, top traders know how to stick around until their best ideas can come to fruition. As one top trader said, "You only have to get rich once."

My hope is that you now have a good foothold—a safe place, from which you can observe the markets knowledgeably, while carving out some profits from your good ideas. As time goes by, you will overcome adversity in the market, and start to develop a real variant perception of your own. By rigorously applying the daily tasks of top traders, you are taking proven steps that will get you from where you are to where you want to be. These are exciting times. By learning about the markets and yourself, you can start to become an entirely new trader. Are you ready to trade with the discipline that will allow you to draw wealth from the markets that could change your life?

Analyst Vs. Trader Vs. Risk Manager

In addition to the twelve tasks—and before we move on to the final chapter—you will find it very helpful to understand the difference between being an analyst, a trader, and a risk manager. In the interbank market, the analyst, the trader and the risk manager are divided into three distinct roles. It is important that you don't mix up these roles:

1. The analyst is responsible for understanding the impact of fundamental data and the technical picture, with a goal of getting the direction correct.

2. The trader is responsible for implementing trades that are in alignment with the analyst's view and for managing open positions, using a combination of prudence and market knowledge. They will decide what levels they want to be in and out at.

3. The risk manager is responsible for making sure position sizes are in alignment with the objectives of the desk, that correlations are kept under control, and that the firm is not over-exposed going into high-volatility news events.

This Distinction Between Roles Is Critical

It is hard for the analyst to remain objective if they have a position on. Or when a trader makes up their own risk-management rules it usually ends up in disaster. This is a challenge for the new breed of retail trader, who needs to be part analyst, part trader, and part risk manager, as well as having to be their own overall business manager. The interbank market has a floor manager who is there to make the different parties play nice (or to fire those who don't perform their role effectively… a luxury the retail trader does not have.

SEGMENT YOUR ACTIVITIES

To help deal with the challenge, you may find it useful to segment your activities along the lines of these three different roles. Your analysis time should be kept separate from your trading time and should allow for an objective assessment of the market, including the positions you have on as a trader. If you start trading at the same time as you analyze the markets, you are likely to get excited and place trades without properly stalking a low-risk entry point.

Your risk-management plan should be developed well in advance of your trading time. The nice thing about risk management is that it is a solvable mathematical problem. It just takes time and thought to make sure your risk-management rules are in alignment with your objectives. You might find it helpful before you start placing trades to imagine that your risk manager has handed you your allocation (and notes on key events)—and if you break these rules today, the floor manager will fire you.

When trading, you can forget about analysis—that should already be done. You should also know exactly how much you are trading. You are simply waiting for your entry conditions to appear, so you can implement the trade(s). You are then monitoring for changes in the market type, levels where the price could reverse, and for events that could change the outlook for the trade. You also conduct prudent risk-management activities to protect profits made.

ALL TEAM MEMBERS ARE JUST AS IMPORTANT AS THE OTHERS

While the trader may want to be the star, their goal is to book the profits for "the team". A trader is a functional cog in a larger trading organization that requires each part to work in sync. This is true even if, in the case of the retail trader, that organization is only one person.

ROLES AND RESPONSIBILITIES OF THE TRADER

To further build on the analyst vs. risk manager vs. trader concept, we can further break down the roles of the trader. In total, these seven roles sketch an accurate picture of an effective trading business. Each one needs to be performed competently for you to be successful.

An accurate framework is also a big help when deciding which roles and responsibilities can be outsourced or automated by the time-poor Forex trader. In addition to the risk manager, trader, and analyst roles, there are four more roles you should be aware of. You may also want to consider how you can outsource some of these duties to relieve some of the time pressure.

Quant/Developer: The quant/developer is responsible for using computers (code) and data to assist in analyzing the markets and automating systems.

Outsourcing: Unless you have a technical proficiency in this area, you may need to outsource any requirements. Look for pre-built solutions, or hire a programmer to complete a job. Note that any costs need to be allocated against your trading profits.

Researcher: The researcher is responsible for generating new trading ideas, edges, and opportunities. They spend their time on system development and updating/improving the market model.

Outsourcing: While it may be tempting to outsource this role, it needs to be done carefully. Buying or learning a system from someone does not always work out, because your system needs to fit you personally before you can trade it properly. Also, the systems you end up buying are often dangerously ignorant of market types.

Psychologist/Performance coach: The psychologist deals with mental issues and peak performance. They help to eliminate self-sabotage and isolate trading problems. They help the trader and business manager set "stretch goals" and support them in achieving them. They help the business manager in holding each role (and the business managers themselves) accountable for performance. They monitor for signs of stress, and make sure the trader is kept in a relaxed state, scheduling breaks when appropriate.

Outsourcing: If possible, I would recommend outsourcing some of this role. Depending on the cost, you may find that a trading group will be able to fulfill some of the required functions.

Business manager: The trading business manager has a multi-faceted role, including record keeping, IT systems, accounting, capital allocation across traders and systems, marketing the trading business/raising funds, broad trading strategy (such as, is it macro, quant, trend-following intra-day, combination) and oversight of the other roles, including accountability for performance. Importantly, the business manager sets goals and objectives for the trading operation.

Outsourcing: The business manager can look to outsource some of the specific duties such as accounting and IT systems. Board strategy, goals, and objectives will need to be kept in house. Accountability can be outsourced to a degree to a coach or group, but ultimate responsibility remains with the business manager. Additionally, look for technology to ease the burden, such as automated software for record keeping.

BALANCING YOUR ROLES

It may seem as if managing these roles is a heavy workload, and it can be. In order to make sure you are being as efficient as possible, it can pay to do a review of your daily activities. In analyzing your activities, you may find you are spending too much time on one area and not enough on others. Perhaps you like trading, so you are always in and out of the market unnecessarily. It could be that you really like being an analyst, so you are constantly going over charts. Perhaps you like system development, so you are constantly working on your trading rules, trying to get them perfect. Think hard about what roles you are over-emphasizing or neglecting, and make conscious adjustments to your schedule. You will likely find that the ones you are neglecting are the ones you need most.

THE CRITICAL ELEMENTS TO MASTERING YOUR TRADING PLAN

"Many people think that trading can be reduced to a few rules. Always do this or always do that. To me, trading isn't about always at all; it is about each situation."

~ Bill Lipschitz

Having a trading plan is critical to being a consistent trader. Without a written plan, emotions almost completely dominate your decisions and experiences when you trade. For instance, when you run into trouble or come across a less-obvious decision point, you can be hijacked by fear or greed. You become irrational and make mistakes. The human limbic system is the gatekeeper for all higher thought processing and evaluation. Your emotions overshadow and prevent logical thought processes. Conversely, when you think rationally and trade your plan, you are in the zone. You're freeing yourself from the constraints of your emotions. You're more open, agreeable, and compliant. All in all, you're much more likely to make much better decisions.

If you have ever traded without a plan, and then started to use one...you'll know the difference is palpable. It's like chalk and cheese. Your plan becomes the foundation for consistent and rational action taking, instead of reckless, emotion-driven mistake making. But not any old plan will do. It needs to be unique and special to you. It needs to be your plan—one you own deep down.

HAVE A TRADING STYLE THAT SUITS YOUR PERSONALITY

"Stick to your own beliefs."

~ Steve Watson

The quest is not finding the one approach that unlocks the secrets to market success but rather finding an approach that fits your personality. You cannot succeed in the markets by copying someone else's approach because the odds are remote that their method will fit your personality. You have to know yourself and not try to be somebody you're not. If you are a day trader, then day trade. If you are a long-term trader, then be a long-term trader. If you are a technician, be one—if you are a macro trader, be exactly that.

Don't get distracted by the number of ideas and strategies you see opportunities in. Be cutthroat, and pick the ones that suit you. Sometimes, this means you have to let go of a promising idea, which is actually okay. Remember, good can be the enemy of great. Don't let it stress you. Note it down, and you can revisit it later if you need to. It's about figuring out what you are the very best at and doing more of those types of trades.

If you want to be as successful as possible in the markets, it stands to reason that you need to zero-in on your winning attributes, and exploit them mercilessly. It's the same in business, art, and even sport. The best of the best know exactly what they're good at and how to use it to full effect. Focus on the strategies, trading vehicles, and time horizons that suit your long-term goals, model of the market, and, importantly, your day-to-day schedule.

THE SEDUCTION OF DAY TRADING

"The less time I am in the market, the less risk I am taking."

~ Mark Minervini

Day trading is like the Vegas of trading. Lots of bright lights and seduction, which only a few seasoned pros can resist well enough to make significant amounts of consistent money from their edge. Now my goal here is not to dissuade you from being a day trader. If you are confident and sure about what you want, you are not going to be persuaded by me, one way or the other. What I do want to do is stop traders from getting stuck down the wrong rabbit hole. Day trading requires enormous amounts of time, preparation, and commitment. This is always going to be beyond the practical reach of many of you.

It is somewhat of a romanticism created by brokers that you can come home in the evening and sit in front of the computer screen, trade, and then pop off to bed with a few grand in profit. Yes, some people can do it, and many other full-time day traders do exist. But these traders are like the professional poker players in Vegas. They are not there on a holiday from their full-time job. It's what they do, day in, day out.

Instead, master the slower timeframes first. Your edge as a retail trader is much greater in swing trading or position trading. Your cost, both in terms of spread and time, are considerably less, and the slower speed cuts down the impact of any mistakes on your performance. Don't think that you need to day trade to make big returns. Less can be more. Carefully consider what you want out of the market, why you have chosen the method you have, and whether it is realistic for you. In saying that, if you want to be a day trader—go for it. You have my full support, and I applaud you for your courage.

HAVE A SIDE INCOME

"I'm extremely well diversified. My thought process is if I screw up in one place, I'll always have a life preserver someplace else."

~ Marty Schwartz

Much of trading effectively is about stress management. A highly stressed trader makes mistakes and has trouble trading their plan. In my first foray into full-time trading, I struggled with this. I knew if I did not make money from my trading, I would not be able to sustain my family and myself. This played havoc with my psyche and led to overtrading. Instead, now, I own businesses and properties that pay me passive income.

These diverse sources of income allow me to manage my stress levels and to commit more capital to my trading. (After you are confident and practiced in your trading system, raising capital becomes one of your biggest challenges.) A wise trader once told me that it does not matter what you do, even if it involves stacking shelves part time. Just make sure you have another source of income if you want to be a trader. Cash flow is king, as it helps you manage stress.

MANAGE YOUR OWN ACCOUNT IF YOU CAN. THERE IS NOTHING LIKE DOING IT

The best way to grow and develop is to live trade. Paper trading, back testing, and trading a demo account all have their uses, but they are very limited since they don't give you the full experience of having skin in the game. Trading is about psychology, and if you neglect this mental component or (much worse) learn bad habits from practice trading, then these "safe" methods of trading can only take you so far.

This is another bad rabbit hole you can all too easily get lost in. Demo trading is a good way to learn the basics of a trading interface, so you don't make mistakes with position sizing or placing orders when you do it for real.

Back testing is valuable in confirming whether a particular technical pattern provides an edge, but it is not going to help you build the best system you possibly can. Think about this: some of the best systems or trades in the world cannot be back tested. It's much better to focus on what is in front of you, rather than dedicate excessive energy to the past.

By being brave, taking the hits, and having the courage to trade live, you take those first steps toward mastery. After that, it is down to hard work, self-awareness, and learning from what you have done in order to become a winner.

KEEP A BALANCED LIFE

"You have to decide whether you want excitement or you want to make money."

~ Mark Cook

"I was totally focused on my trading. Not my health. Not my relationships."

~ Jimmy Balodimas

If you recall our chapter on the tasks of master traders, one task we missed (kudos to you if you noticed it) was the task of being out of the market. An unhealthy or unbalanced obsession with any activity is not conducive to long-term success. If you recall, Van Tharp suggests we are made up of a mess of conflicting parts. Each of your parts has good intentions, but if you don't take steps to satisfy those parts outside of trading, they will have no other option but to interfere with your trading processes.

If you don't satisfy your need for excitement outside of the market, for example, then you may try to satisfy it when you are trading (with disastrous consequences). The market is not there for pleasure. It is therefore important to learn to deal with your personal issues outside of the market. In a sense, you can hang them on the metaphorical "coat rack" when you sit down to trade, and then pick them up again when you finish for the day. You should also schedule vacation time, and take breaks during the day.

TRADE IN ALIGNMENT WITH YOUR PURPOSE

"I don't judge success. I celebrate it. I think success has to do with finding and following ones calling regardless of financial gain."

~ Ed Seykota

The best traders understand their greater role in the trading ecology. They know why they are trading (outside of simply "making money"), and are appreciative of the good they create—both in their own lives and others'—through their trading activities. Acknowledgement of your purpose is an important check to the hubris of success. If you let your wins get to you, you start to think you are bigger than the market—a sure invitation for a costly comeuppance. Understanding and valuing your purpose keeps your ego in check.

On the flip side, being clear about the good you are doing is a critical factor in aligning your subconscious toward wealth. When you know your role deep down, and you can see the bigger picture, it helps to eliminate some of the subtler forms of self-sabotage, such as the negative attitude toward wealth that many people have as a result of their upbringing ("rich people are selfish," etc.).

IMPORTANT TOOLS TO HAVE ON HAND WHEN YOU TRADE

When you trade, you want to have some resources ready on hand. These will help you to eliminate mistakes, and keep your trading psychology in ship sharp shape.

FILL OUT THE TRADING PLAN TEMPLATE

Complete the trading plan template. You may need to refer back to earlier lessons to fill out some of the sections.

Don't trade without a written plan.

You can get the template for free here when you subscribe to the course based on this book:

www.fxrenew.com/forex-course

WRITE YOUR TRADING PRINCIPLES

You want to keep a summary of your trading principles on hand, so you can refer to it easily. It is good to refresh yourself often, and to review your performance against them as well.

CREATE A TRADING CHECKLIST

A trading checklist is what you refer to each day—to ensure you are following correct trading processes. You will write your trading checklist as part of your daily/weekly trading routine.

THANK YOU AND WHERE TO FROM HERE

"A losing trader can do little to transform himself into a winning trader. A losing trader is not going to want to transform himself. That's the kind of thing winning traders do."

~ Ed Seykota

"Anything is possible with persistence and hard-work. It can be done, and your own determination to succeed is the most important element."

~ Bill O'Neil

You have made it to the end of **The Consistent Trader**... but your journey is only just beginning. Firstly, I want to say thank you for the considerable time and effort you have put into reading this book. Making it to the end is a real achievement to be proud of. Secondly, I would love to hear any feedback you have regarding the book and how your trading has changed based on what you've learned in this book.

Please contact me on **sam@fxrenew.com**.

Want trading ideas direct to your inbox?

FX Renew was developed to give you, the retail trader, access to the ideas and signals of ex-bank and industry traders. They are traders with a wealth of market savvy that just can't be matched in the modern day and age, where banks are shutting down their prop trading desks. Their signals and insights are clear, actionable, and provide an immersive learning experience. Get your free trial here:

www.fxrenew.com/choose-your-subscription

Continue the conversation?

I publish my best work each week on the FX Renew Blog. If you are not a member already and want to continue to receive trading inspiration and insight, I suggest you join the FX Renew blog. It's your secret weapon to becoming a winning Forex trader—and it's free.

Know other traders?

If you like what you have read in this book, why not share it with other traders you know?

Thanks again, and take care.

Cheers,

Sam

APPENDIX 1, A MONTH OF DAY TRADES, THE ADVANCED FOREX COURSE IN ACTION

I built a trading system to showcase in practice the concepts in this book. It is a day trading system designed to trade breakouts around the European open, using the 15-minute chart.

Here is its verified live performance:

Weekly return	Monthly return	Profit factor	History
+4.8%	+21.9%	1.92	34 days

There are a few notable points about the performance of the system:

- The initial stop-loss was only hit once (and only with 1/3 of a position)
- The largest loss was less than 1R
- Only 1 loss was greater than 0.5R
- The largest winner was 2.4R
- There were 5 winners greater than 1R
- The total sum of all losses was only just greater than the single largest winning trade
- I cost myself 3.3R in mistakes (-13%!)

I am quite happy with the way the system works. It keeps losses small, let's profits run, and has the potential for very large winners every now and again.

SYSTEM DEVELOPMENT, PART 1, HOW I DEVELOPED THE SYSTEM

It's pretty obvious that trends often breakout around the European open on some currency pairs. Traders are asleep, they go to work, bringing a whole lot more volume into the market, and it starts to trend.

Because lots of smart people know this, there will be false breakouts where the price reverses.

So I had the choice of either trading the breakout or fading the breakout. For this system, I chose trading with it (due to personal preference).

That means the system's job is to capture the breakout, and make the most of it, and to limit any losses if the breakout is false. I chose a set of rules that were appropriate, and put it together in a plan by back testing on the charts. I then started to trade it live. I wanted to place 20 trades exactly per my rules (about a months' worth of trading), and then if it showed promise, review the performance. You can see a visual record of all the trades I placed below.

(Note that at the end of the month, the workload was too great for me to continue to run the system each day as I also am heavily involved in our trading signals. You can view the performance of the signals here. I now run the system every now and again when I have the time to focus on it).

SYSTEM DEVELOPMENT, PART 2, HOW TO IMPROVE THE SYSTEM

The next stage of system development is where it gets interesting. After 20 trades on a discretionary system, you start to get an idea about what is working and what is not (if it is a mechanical system, you need a lot more). To assist in my analysis, I run my system's live results though FX Blue's free analyzer service.

This is quite useful, but also it is not a perfect solution, as my scaling in and out approach does not work well with the software (I think I need to tag my trades with a magic number in future to assist here).

Here are some stats on the trades:

Returns						
Total return:	23.10%					
Banked return:	23.10%					
Per day:	0.95%	Per active day:	1.16%	Arithmetic mean:	1.28%	
Per week:	4.84%					
Per month:	21.94%					

Balance				
Worst day %	Worst week %	Worst month %	Deepest valley	Loss from outset
-5.4%	-2.4%	+9.5%	-7.4%	-.--

Equity (approximate)				
Worst day %	Worst week %	Worst month %	Deepest valley	Loss from outset
-5.4%	-2.4%	-.--	-7.4%	-.--

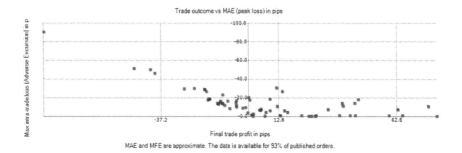

Trade outcome vs MAE (peak loss) in pips

MAE and MFE are approximate. The data is available for 93% of published orders.

Here are a few points to note:

- 7 trades were winners, 8 were losers, and 7 were breakeven.

- I was most profitable trading the EURUSD and the GBPUSD (all the other pairs I traded were either losing or breakeven). You can see this information in FX Blue.

- I missed some trends on the EURUSD and the GBPUSD because I had "spent my bullets" trading other pairs.

- Most of my mistakes had to do with the re-entry.

- I did not make profit on Mondays on average. (Also in FX Blue.)

- In general, trading in direction of the trend would have produced better results. (I get this by looking at the charts.)

- So from the data, and from anything else I noticed, I can then decide if I want to make any changes to my system.

Here are some changes I could make.

- I will cut my re-entry size to 50%

- I will only enter in the direction indicated by my daily market type analysis. (Alternatively, I could put a 100 x 5 displaced moving average on the chart, and only trade long if the price is above that or short if the price is below that).

- I am still going to continue to trade on Mondays.

As you can see, it is really just common sense. My job now is to execute my plan exactly per my new rules for the next 20 trades, and see what happens.

TRADES IN DETAIL

Losses:

-0.13R

-0.31R

-0.15R

-0.28R

-0.30R

-0.49R

-0.25R

-0.83R (when the trailing stop was hit after scaling-in)

Winners:

+0.57R

+0.26R

+1.57R

+1.52R

+2.40R

+1.13R

+1.29R

The rest of the trades came in at roughly breakeven (plus or minus less than 0.1R). Here are the charts of the trades. My marking up is not that great now I look back on it, so here are some pointers.

- An up or down allow indicates an entry at the close of the candle (where I have drawn the red line)

- A sideways arrow indicates where I have closed part of the position

- When I close a trade, I am closing a fraction of the remaining position. So if I close 1/3, it means I am closing 1/3 of whatever I have in the market at that time.

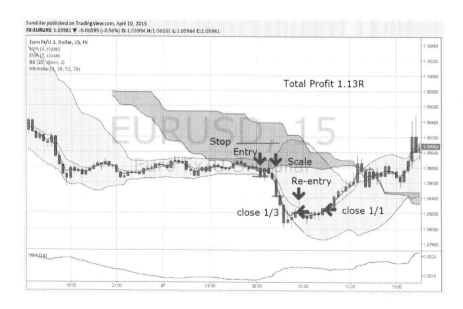

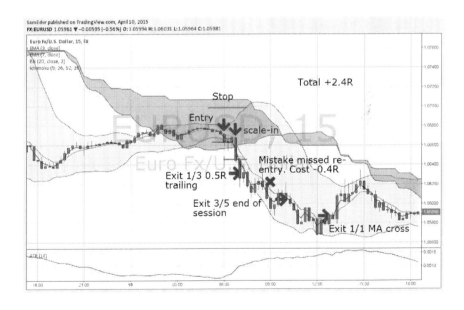

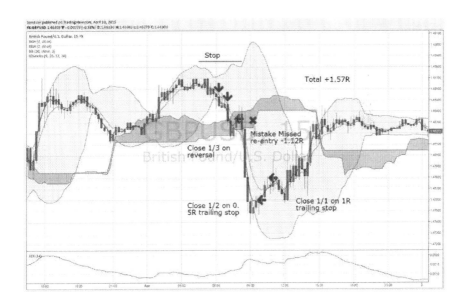

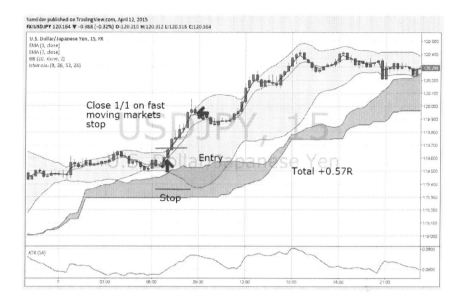

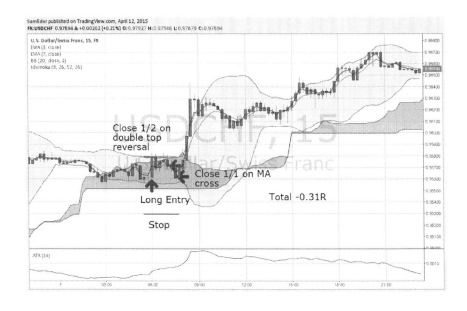

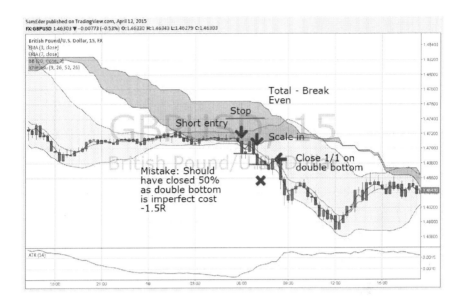

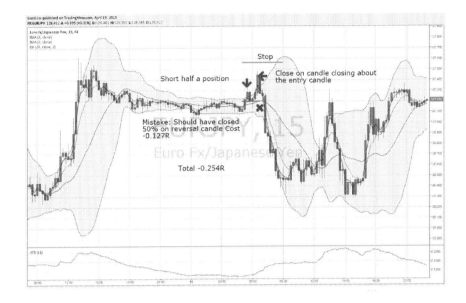

COMPLETE SYSTEM RULES

This system can be used on a variety of timeframes and markets. The principles are universal, but it will need adapting to the specific timeframe and market traded. The below rules are based off the 15-minute timeframe.

First, you want to do your big-picture analysis, and choose your favorite currency pairs for the day. Look for the daily market type to be trending in your direction and higher timeframe candlesticks that point to a direction for the day (such as a daily breakout or reversal candle). You can also assess fundamental sentiment and correlations. To make this easier for you, each week I post my big-picture analysis on the FX Renew blog.

Scan your favored currency pairs, and look for either a sideways quiet or sideways normal market type just prior to the European open (the time you trade is key, so don't miss this part).

Double check for any major news events. Avoid trading around major news events only.

Wait for one of two entry conditions:

Trend following: The close of a candle outside the upper or lower Bollinger Band in the direction of the trend.

Reversal: A reversal candle (hammer, engulfing, etc.) in the direction of the trend.

Once you have entered, measure the distance between the upper and mid Bollinger Band. Place your stop this distance behind the Bollinger Band that is not in the direction of your trend. So if you are buying, place the stop below the lower Bollinger Band, and vice versa if you are selling.

If trading a breakout from a sideways quiet MT, then scale-in the first bullish candle after entry, and tighten the stop so you are risking the same amount (aggressive or high-conviction traders can scale-in three times).

If you get a reversal candle right after the entry, close 1/2 your position.

For reversal trades, if the price closes above your entry candle, then trail the stop to the high of the candle (or simply exit).

Close 1/3 of your position on the first reversal candle, or alternatively, close 1/3 of your position on a profit target placed on the first resistance/support level.

If the market moves fast in your favor, then close at least 2/3 on the first bearish close back inside the Bollinger Bands.

Close the second 1/3 of your position on a minor double top or bottom.

Close the position on a cross of the 3-period and 7-period exponential moving averages (this can be ignored if still inside the initial entry range).

Close out at the end of the trading session, or apply a tight (1 or 0.5R), automated trailing stop and hold.

SOME TIPS AND SUGGESTIONS

You can close out the entire position on a minor double top or bottom.

To capture longer trends, you can trail the stop on the super-trend indicator rather than the 3-period and 7-period moving averages.

If the big picture dictates, you can switch to the 1-hour timeframe to trail the final 1/3 of the position. You can take a small position at market on the open in the direction you favor for the day.

Rather than exit at market, you can trail your stop to the low or high of the candle. This will allow your profits to run just that little bit more.

Don't put your stop too tight!

Focus on being happy and relaxed when you are trading.

Don't try to be perfect in your entries and exits.

It may take a month or two to get used to trading the system. Persevere.

Once you have some experience trading this system, feel free to adapt it to fit your style. Don't be afraid to use your common sense and experience!

Appendix 2, Free Trial: The New Pathway

In the past, if you wanted to become a trader, you would get a job at a major bank. The aspiring trader would be chucked in the deep end with an order book, and those smart and determined enough would survive to grow into accomplished traders in their own right.

How Did They Learn?

There was no textbook; it was actually about the people. If they were lucky enough, the new entrant would befriend some wise, old trader who would act as a mentor of sorts. But really, they learned through a kind of osmosis—by being around people who knew what they were doing—absorbing what worked and figuring out how to fit it to their trading style. Today, that pathway is gone. Banks aren't hiring or are closing down their desks. Now is the new age of the retail trader.

But how do you, as the heir apparent, master the skills you need to survive without access to the traditional bank way?

It's Not Easy

It took me seven years, and it was not until a chance encounter with an ex-bank trader, who took me under his wing and introduced me to other bank and hedge fund traders, that I really began to get a handle on what it takes to trade well—and start producing results. Forget indicators. Forget news and opinions. What you really need to learn is access to the right *people*.

This Is What We Do

We give you access. Access to traders who have been there and done that. And it's done in an actionable way. You are watching people actually do it in a manner you can follow and generate returns from.

When you start your free trial, you immediately begin to receive signals from ex-bank and industry traders. Each trade comes with entry and exit rules, and more importantly, the reason behind the trade.

On top of this, you get direct access to our traders in the chat-room, so you can have all that experience at your fingertips. It does not stop there. In addition, you get access to our training course, technical analysis lessons, and custom position-sizing algorithms.

And let's not forget our Forex System Development Workshop.

Get your free trial of FX Renew:

www.fxrenew.com/choose-your-subscription

ABOUT THE AUTHOR

Sam Eder is a macro currency trader who has been featured on FX Street, Forexlive, and Market Wizard Van Tharp's website. He is an ex-army officer and holds a master's degree in leadership. Sam is the owner of FX Renew, a Forex business providing signals and education from ex-bank and industry traders. Over 3000 traders have been through his acclaimed Advanced Forex Course for Smart Traders, and this is his first book covering the art and science of Forex trading.

Book Discounts and Special Deals

Sign up for free to get discounts
and special deals on our best-selling books at

www.TCKPublishing.com/bookdeals

Made in the USA
Columbia, SC
30 September 2018